DREAM AGAIN

A Story of Faith, Courage, and the Tenacity to Overcome

ISAIAH AUSTIN

WITH MATT LITTON

FOREWORD BY ROBERT GRIFFIN III

HOWARD BOOKS

An Imprint of Simon & Schuster, Inc.

New York   Nashville   London   Toronto   Sydney   New Delhi

Howard Books
An Imprint of Simon & Schuster, Inc.
1230 Avenue of the Americas
New York, NY 10020

First Howard Books hardcover edition June 2015

HOWARD and colophon are trademarks of Simon & Schuster, Inc.

For information about special discounts for bulk purchases,
please contact Simon & Schuster Special Sales at 1-866-506-1949
or business@simonandschuster.com.

The Simon & Schuster Speakers Bureau can bring authors
to your live event. For more information or to book an event,
contact the Simon & Schuster Speakers Bureau at 1-866-248-3049
or visit our website at www.simonspeakers.com.

Interior design by Davina Mock-Maniscalco

Manufactured in the United States of America

10   9   8   7   6   5   4   3   2   1

Library of Congress Control Number: 2015005201

ISBN 978-1-5011-0739-9
ISBN 978-1-5011-0740-5 (ebook)

CONTENTS

CONTENTS

FOREWORD BY ROBERT GRIFFIN III

I first met Isaiah Austin in my last year on campus at Baylor University while he was still early in his high school basketball career. I've always loved the game of basketball, so when I wasn't on the football field, I was often hanging around the gym and enjoying the program that Coach Drew was in the early stages of rebuilding. Isaiah was the highest-rated prep player in the country at the time, and he had just committed to play basketball as a Baylor Bear. When Isaiah began to visit campus more often, he and I kindled a new friendship. I was impressed with his competitive spirit, his sense of humor, and his genuine concern for other people.

I watched Isaiah deal with the pressures and expectations of arriving on campus as the highest-level basketball recruit to ever commit to Baylor. I respected how he took care of the things that really mattered: handling his business on campus, making good grades, and always treating people with respect. I watched him grow and mature from a highly rated recruit who struggled a bit through his freshman season into a talented and confident leader in his second year who helped lead his team deep into the NCAA tournament.

I knew nothing about Isaiah's eye problems and everything he had overcome to be one of the elite college players in the country. We talked regularly through his time on campus, and never did he mention that he was blind in one eye. As someone who grew up playing basketball, it was astonishing to me that he overcame those challenges to become such a dominant presence on the court. When Isaiah began talking openly to the team and to the media about his vision impairment, my respect for him grew even greater. He never wanted anyone to make excuses for him. He just wanted to compete. I admired him as a person and as an athlete, but like millions of others who watched the feature about him or read his interviews, I was also inspired by my friend's toughness and determination to succeed.

As the 2014 NBA draft approached, Isaiah had put himself in the position to be a role model and inspiration to others. I was excited for him to make an impact in the league. I turned on ESPN one Sunday morning to learn the terrible news that Marfan syndrome would end Isaiah's career. Many of his friends from the Baylor family and I tried to encourage him through that time, but in true Isaiah form, we found that he was too busy encouraging us. Even with his lifelong dream crashing down around him, Isaiah was focused on others.

What happened to Isaiah would have crushed many people. When something so catastrophic happens, it can make you question everything around you. But it can also bring you closer to God. I already had so much respect for what Isaiah had accomplished as a person and as an athlete. Watching how he dealt with losing the one thing he had worked so hard for his entire life made me appreciate him even more for his great faith in God.

People talk about how Isaiah "lost his dream," but as his friend I have learned to see it differently. This is why everyone should read this book: we all have dreams that are important to us. Most of us can relate to how hard it is when things happen and those dreams slip away. But very few people I've known understand what it means or what it requires to really dream again.

Isaiah Austin has a lot to teach us about the toughness, faith, and trust in God it takes to find new dreams. I truly believe that Isaiah's faith has placed him right where God needs him the most. I think my friend's story has the power to inspire you, strengthen your faith, and help you learn what it means to dream again in your life.

—Robert Griffin III

DREAM AGAIN

CHAPTER 1

BLINDSIDED

I am seven feet tall, so I stand out everywhere I go. Each time I shop at the mall, every time I get out of my car at a gas station, anytime I walk across campus at school, people notice me. Standing out or being different is something I've just had to deal with my whole life. But it's not my height that really makes me different from everyone else in the world; it's my *vision*.

Let me explain. I take great pride in how well I see the game of basketball, especially when I am out there competing on the court. I can see a teammate coming open off a cut before he's actually open. I'll beat you to the ball because I can see on which side of the paint a rebound is going to fall before the shot is missed. I can tell if a double team is coming to trap me in the post before it actually gets to me. I've worked hard all my life to see these things better than other players.

But there are a lot of guys out there who work hard to have that kind of vision on the court. So when I talk about "the way I see," I am also talking about something much bigger. I strive to have a *life vision*. Life vision is similar to vision on the court, but instead of being all about the game, it's all about how well you can visualize your dreams. My whole life I've tried to look toward the positive, even in the worst circumstances, and I see my dreams coming true.

From the time I was five years old living in California, I had a vision of playing in the NBA. I know a lot of other kids might say that kind of thing, but this was different. Even when I was a child, I could see myself on the stage at Radio City Music Hall on draft night. I could visualize every part—I could see myself dressed in a crisp suit, sitting at a table with my family, hugging my mom and dad when my name was called, walking up those stairs to shake hands with the commissioner, taking the franchise hat, smiling for the cameras, and letting my personality shine while I did the post-draft interviews. For as long as I can remember, I could see all of those details clearly when I laid my head down on the pillow at night, when I woke up in the morning, every time I took the court, and each time I stood on my driveway to practice the game I love so much. That vision drove me to where I am today; it made me the person I am right now. Although I've had a difficult time seeing the details in my everyday life that most people take for granted, I could still *always* see my dream.

A big part of my story is about dreams and what it takes to make them come true. That kind of vision comes from hard work, grinding it out every day, especially on the days when I didn't feel like working. It comes from the support of family, learning to overcome adversity, and staying positive, even when everything in the world around me was negative. I think that's one of the reasons why I've always liked the Bible character Joseph. Every time my preacher would talk about Joseph, he'd talk about dreams. I could identify with Joseph because even when things were tough for him, when he was in trouble, separated from his family, and no one else believed in him, he still held on to his vision; he still kept his dreams in sight.

Since God gave Joseph his dreams, Joseph knew that meant they would come true. And just the same for me, I believed God had given me this dream of playing in the NBA and it was destined to be true.

FIVE DAYS BEFORE the 2014 NBA draft, I woke up early with my heart beating fast. Leading up to this big day, I had traveled to NBA franchises all over the country and competed as hard as I could through eleven different workouts. I checked my phone when I got out of bed that morning to reread the messages from my agent, Dwon Clifton, who had received great news from one of my last workouts with the Los Angeles Clippers.

After a great sophomore season at Baylor, which included a Sweet 16 appearance in the NCAA tournament, I made the difficult decision to leave college at the end of season and enter my name into the draft. My head coach, Scott Drew, along with the rest of the Baylor coaching staff, helped me make the best possible decision and then supported and encouraged me once my choice was final. Still, a lot of people doubted my decision to come out of college early. The experts said I wasn't ready. Early on in the process I attended the NBA combine and was flagged to do some testing on my heart, so several of the scouts had me going late in the second round and a lot of people even had me projected as going undrafted. But I knew it was my time. I can't explain it any better than that. I didn't necessarily want to leave the campus I loved so much, but I had this gut feeling that it was my moment to go.

Throughout the whole pre-draft process, I only had one terrible performance, and that was mainly because I had been sick with some type of flu. My energy was low for the workout, and I know it had a huge effect on how I played that afternoon. There were a few moments where things didn't look good, but I stayed positive and kept hanging on to my vision. The truth is that the more I played and interviewed for teams, the better news my agent seemed to be getting. There were several teams who were interested in taking me with their first-round pick.

In addition to wanting to see my dream fulfilled, I also felt I had something to prove about myself and my ability. I had a pretty big chip on my shoulder because of the lack of respect I got as a player all season—even when my numbers and performances were consistently better than some of the guys who were projected to be solid first-round draft picks. I knew when all the talk was done, when we were in the gym going at it, I was going to rise to the top. I never let the doubters get me down, though—in fact, they drove me to work even harder. I stayed focused, and sure enough, my name continued to climb higher on the draft board, even ahead of players who had gotten a lot more hype than me during the college season.

When my agent called that Friday morning with great news from the Clippers, I was so excited. They told him that I shot the ball better than a lot of guards they had already tried out. They liked how energetic I was around the basket, how versatile I was for a seven-foot player, and how good my passing and dribbling were for a guy my size. They said I was very skilled and that they thought they could help me put some weight on and that I might be a great fit in their program. The NBA is big business and there are no guarantees, but the Clippers had a late first-round pick. They were a veteran team, and my agent believed it would be a great place for me to develop my game and learn from the best. We had gotten this kind of feedback from a couple of other teams, and I started to believe I had a legitimate shot at the first round. I ate breakfast thinking about those texts, the Clippers, playing on the same team with guys like Chris Paul and Blake Griffin, being coached by a future Hall of Fame guy like Doc Rivers . . . I imagined playing in front of thousands of fans and even Hollywood movie stars sitting courtside to watch every game. I was thinking about what it meant to be a first-rounder after I had spent my whole college career with people on the outside, criticizing and doubting my ability. It was hard not to be too excited. But I had to stay focused. I was about to head to Chicago, another solid team with a great coach and a lot of veterans, for my final workout the next morning. That's right, the Bulls, the team that one of my idols, Michael Jordan, helped lead to six championships.

MY HIGH SCHOOL coach and mentor, Coach Ray, picked me up early to head over to Mo Williams's gym. I have known Ray since

I was a sophomore in high school. He was one of the best coaches in the Dallas area, and he had introduced me to Mo, who has been in the league since 2003 and has even played in the All-Star game. He's not only a close friend of mine, but he has also taken me under his wing and taught me a lot about the game. He knows all about the business of what it takes to prepare physically and mentally for the NBA, and he let me train at his gym to get myself ready for the draft. Mo calls his place the Mo Williams Academy. It has a weight room, some turfs for pushing and pulling sleds to strengthen my legs, and a full-court regulation gym. Like a lot of other great players from the Dallas area, the Academy had been my lab; it was the place where I had prepared for my dream for years. If I wasn't in Waco with my Baylor family, I was usually at Mo's working out on my own or with the athletes who went there to improve their game and get bigger and stronger and faster.

Ray and I met up with my trainers, Jay Jackson and Keith Sweat, and walked into the gym laughing and talking about the good news from LA and feeling hopeful about the week ahead. I had already shaken off the cobwebs following my flights from Dallas to LA to Toronto and back home all in one week. That kind of travel was just a little taste of the NBA grind I would experience during my upcoming rookie season. Jay and Sweat are like brothers to me. Jay had played college basketball in Mississippi and was Mo's personal trainer. Sweat was an awesome coach who was really helping me develop my ball-handling skills—something that separated me from other big guys. They had closed down the Academy that day so we could do our work without getting interrupted. Once we hit the floor, Ray did what he always does: he helped me focus my vision on the next play. Yeah, my dreams were close, but it wasn't time to celebrate just yet; it was time to go to work and prepare for my tryout in Chicago.

Everybody told me it would be a "light" day at the gym. Ray is always coming up with new footwork and shooting drills and pulling new stuff together for me from watching tape of NBA great Hakeem Olajuwon, so his workouts are never boring. They said they wanted to make sure that I was fresh when I hit the court for my last tryout, in Chicago, but every time I get on the court I look at it as a chance to get better, so I never want to take it easy. I went hard through my shooting workouts: post moves, free throws, jump shots, threes, and then I finished up on the court with some ball-handling drills. Even though it was all pretty routine, Jay and Sweat made it interesting and fun, as usual—so I never felt bored with the kind of "normal" workout I had probably done a couple thousand times. Jay even made me do some light work in the weight room for a while before I finished up and hit the showers. I'm not sure I could've imagined at that moment how different my whole life would be the next time I stepped onto the basketball court at Mo's Academy. We stood around and talked for a few minutes about my upcoming trip to

Chicago, and then Coach Ray got a call to invite us all over to Mo's house and kick it for the rest of the day.

I rode with Ray across town to Mo's house, and we got there early in the afternoon. It was perfect weather, a great day to be outside, and Mo was hanging out with his wife and kids in the backyard grilling up his usual feast. Mo can cook just as well as he can play ball. Jay and Sweat drove over, too, and we spent the day talking about life and relaxing. Mo has some great experiences from his time as a professional basketball player, and getting to listen to him tell stories about the league and what he's learned is priceless. Whenever he talks, believe me, I am taking notes.

One of my favorite things about going to Mo's house is getting to hang out with his five kids. I have been around little kids my whole life. Growing up, I was the oldest and Mom would always put me in charge of babysitting my little brother and sister and sometimes watching over our neighbor's kids, too. To tell you the truth, one of my favorite things to do when I am not playing basketball is to be "the big brother." Kids are so full of joy and energy. It is relaxing to take a break from all the competition and focus my attention on them instead of the next thing I have to do, the next place I have to be, or the next drill I've got to win. That's why I've always loved hanging with the kids and teaching at camps. If there is a place away from the court I feel most comfortable, it is working with kids. Mo's crew of little ones and I played video games and then went out to the driveway to play basketball. I was doing different dunks for them and lifting their little bodies so they could jam the ball in the basket. Mainly, I was goofing off and making them laugh. I remember thinking that it was a perfect day hanging around people who have become like family to me.

Ray felt it was time to head out around eight o'clock that night, and he offered to drive me over to my aunt Evelyn's house. I remember him saying he had to make a call before we left. He walked out to the driveway by himself and seemed to be having a serious conversation on his phone while I said good-bye to Mo and his family. I was staying with my aunt Evelyn and uncle Dre in Dallas a lot that summer because it was closer to the airport and the Academy. Evelyn and Dre are great people who love to laugh and play games, and they have been part of my family since I was a freshman in high school. They aren't my aunt and uncle by blood, but over the years their house has become my second home.

I wanted to be rested and ready for my last NBA workout in Chicago so I could finish strong. Coach Ray and I talked a lot on that long drive from Mo's to my aunt's house. We were messing around with each other and laughing, listening to music, and having a good conversation. Ray and I text each other almost every day, so he pretty much knows about everything going on in my life. I wouldn't be who I am today without him. He always tells me the truth and keeps me grounded; he's taught me so much about staying focused on my dreams.

As we drove, Ray asked how I was feeling about the whole interview process and my tryouts. I was hyped and busy talking about how ready I was for Chicago and how excited I was about the draft on Thursday, but I clearly remember that he interrupted something that I was saying and told me how proud he was of me. Coach Ray and I have a lot of history; he's been with me through so many tough times. He told me he was proud of me for the way I had been maturing on and off the court. And I still remember his last comment on our drive together. He said very seriously that no matter what happened he knew I was going to be all right. Everything was going to be okay.

The car got real quiet, and I closed my eyes, thinking about how close it all was to being real. In just five short days, I'd be there in New York City. I had already chosen my suit. My parents; my fifteen-year-old younger brother, Noah; and my eleven-year-old sister, Narah; Coach Ray; my agent Dwon; and Coach Drew (from Baylor) would all be sitting around that table with me. My man Cory Jefferson was going to be there, too, with his people. Cory was my teammate at Baylor and had become a really good friend. It was going to be a great night for both of us. The commissioner, Adam Silver, would walk up on the stage and call my name just how I had always envisioned it. And the best part was: I just knew in my heart it was going to happen in the first round. That's right, prime-time TV. ESPN. I knew I was going to get called; the only question I had left in my mind was which franchise hat I would be putting on when I posed with the commissioner for that photo. I could almost hear the announcement: "With the next pick in the NBA draft . . ." Would it be the Clippers? The Bulls? The Celtics? The Spurs? I believed that God had given me this dream. It was my dream and I had done my part. He was finally going to deliver. Like I said, the only real question was which team's hat it was going to be.

WE TURNED ONTO Aunt Evelyn and Uncle Dre's street. Usually, when I go over there to stay, there are only two cars in the driveway, but I noticed that there were way too many cars parked up and down the road and near their house. Aunt Evelyn loves to have a party, but this had to be something really big, and I hadn't heard them say anything about it all week. It was dark outside, but as we got closer I realized that my aunt's driveway was also packed full of cars. Finally, I noticed my mom and dad's car parked outside their house. I sat back and looked at Ray and wondered why my parents had made the long drive down from Kansas City. I knew how busy they had been with work and my brother's and sister's activities. We had gotten such great news about the draft in the past few days that maybe it really was a party. Maybe we were all going to be celebrating Thursday together just a little bit early.

Ray told me to go on into the house. As I got out of the car and began to walk up the driveway, I heard him turn off the car engine and realized that he wasn't just dropping me off. He parked his car in front of their mailbox and also walked toward the house. I turned to look at him and noticed that Jay and Sweat had followed us from Mo's and were getting out of their cars.

Something was going on that I had not seen.

I remember asking Ray, "What's going on? Why are Jay and Sweat here, too? Are we having a party or something?" The expression on his face was different; it was really serious, like all of a sudden his mood had changed. I was more concerned than confused now. Ray put his hand on my shoulder and had me walk alongside him up the sidewalk toward the front porch. We stood there for just a moment in the quiet while I tried to get my mind around what could be happening.

I opened the door and walked into the long foyer. Even with all the cars sitting outside, I was surprised to see the house full of so many people that I call my family. The living room in Aunt Evelyn's house is very bright and just barely hidden to the right of the foyer. I remember each step I took as clearly as I remember anything that has ever happened to me in my life. I can still see it all in slow motion—every terrible detail. One look at the faces of the people I loved and I knew this wasn't a party. It was dead silent. I started looking from person to person and noticed my guys from Baylor: Coach Tang, Coach Mills, Coach McCasland, Coach Drew, Coach Maloney, and then I realized it was *all* of them—the entire staff was sitting along the left side of the room. Both of my pastors were also there, and as I moved toward a full view of the living room, I could see that it was completely jam-packed with people, standing-room only. I looked at my cousins Kristina and Ron, Uncle Dre, my girlfriend, my agent, Coach Pops, my dad, my brother and sister, too many people to name . . . and after scanning all of those concerned faces, I finally saw Mom.

I was really thrown off by the sight of Mom. My mom is my inspiration. She has always been my biggest fan. She's the light of my world, always smiling and staying positive no matter what happens. She had her hands over her eyes, but I could see the tears dripping down her cheeks. When she brought her hands down, her eyes were red, like she had been crying all day.

The pain in her expression was terrible. Had something bad happened to someone in the family? The last time I'd seen people this sad was when my grandfather, my mom's dad, had passed away. I kept looking around, my mind racing and my heart beating fast—the way it does when you feel like something really bad is going down.

I can't remember exactly what I said at that moment. I looked at Mom and started to shake my head. Maybe if I didn't believe it, maybe it wouldn't be real. She put her hands back over her face. The whole room was so quiet that I was sure everybody could hear me breathing. Finally, my mom looked at me and said, "I am so sorry, Isaiah." At that point, most of the room was in tears. I remember my little brother and sister, my coaches, pastors, and all of these people I loved were crying. I looked around, still shaking my head, but this was real.

Like I told you earlier, my vision has always been a big deal to me; my whole life I have worked hard to overcome so much and had taken pride in how well I see, but this news . . . this was something that I never saw coming. I knew exactly what my mom was saying.

I had tested positive for Marfan syndrome. It is a condition that I didn't fully understand at that moment, but I knew what it meant for my dream. I leaned over and put my hands on my knees feeling like someone had knocked the breath right out of my chest.

It was the test the doctors made me take weeks ago at the NBA combine in Chicago. The NBA doctors had thought that my heart was enlarged, which wasn't unusual for someone as tall as me. They sent my blood work off for some evaluations and said I had a fifty-fifty chance of having a condition that could end my career. This news initially dropped me from the first-round projections. Still, I went through the draft tryouts and focused on my vision. I thought I had overcome it. I had been through similar tests as a kid and they had all come back okay. No one in my family has a history of Marfan syndrome, which is a genetic disorder. I had played basketball my whole life with no heart issues at all. In fact, I was in the best physical condition of my life. I was supposed to walk across the stage on draft night. I didn't even waste time or energy worrying about their test. I did what Joseph from the Bible would've done: I trusted God and kept my focus on the work in front of me.

I stood there for a moment in shock. This couldn't be true. I had left it in God's hands, which meant I had trusted that He would take care of me. I was sure it was God who had given me this dream when I was a kid. I kept my faith and worked through so much adversity to get to this moment. I was five days from that vision coming true. And now, in that moment, I felt hopeless. I remember looking over my shoulder toward the door because part of me wanted to run away. Like maybe if I could get away from the house, none of this would be true. I looked back and Coach Ray and the guys were blocking the door in a way that made it obvious they weren't going to let me get by them. I looked around the room and everybody seemed to be watching me to see what I would do next.

All of a sudden I couldn't get my breath. I leaned my head against the wall for a moment and then it really hit me. I felt every bit like somebody should feel when they dream, they work, they overcome, they stay focused on one goal their whole life, and in an instant, it all comes crashing down around them. Yet here I was, surrounded by the most important people in my life. These were the people who dreamed with me, taught me how to fight, to persevere, and to be a man. They were the people I would want by my side on draft night. That's where we were all supposed to be together—celebrating in New York on Thursday, hearing family and fans cheer me on as I stood on that stage after hearing my name called. But instead I found myself at the center of a stage I never wanted—with my loved ones staring at me as I heard the worst news of my life and began to feel my whole world crashing down on me.

And in that moment, before I knew what was happening, I just fell to the floor. It was as if everything went fuzzy for a couple of minutes. My friends on the Baylor football team talk about getting blindsided on the field with a tackle you never see coming, but the same thing can happen on the basketball court. Basketball is a really physical game. It moves so fast that there is an important rule out there when you are playing with your team, a trust you have to have in your teammates: if a player from the other team comes to hit you with a screen, one of your guys will talk to you and yell out a warning. Many times you are too busy guarding your man and taking care of your own business to see that big screen coming. You are completely dependent on the voices of your teammates to avoid a big hit. I've seen guys knocked out by a screen they didn't know was coming their way. It hasn't happened to me often, but I've been blindsided on the court a couple of times and it was never fun. That's the best way to describe how I felt at that moment in Aunt Evelyn's house. As if life had blindsided me—hard. I felt like no one had talked to me, no one had given me a warning. I stayed down on the floor with my head in my hands, and for the first time in my life, I really cried about losing my dream.

I began talking to God. Why had He brought me this far, only to be handed such a terrible diagnosis? I kept hearing my mom's words, "I am so sorry, Isaiah," run through my mind. I could hear my aunt crying. I think people were getting up from around the living room. But I just couldn't see it. After fighting for a vision my entire life, I couldn't bear to look around.

I said earlier that life vision is about how well you can see your dreams. For twenty years, I had learned how to see the positive, to visualize my dreams coming true, even when circumstances had made those dreams harder to see. I had overcome so much to get to this point. I took a deep breath and covered my left eye, wiping away a tear. In my mind, I kept asking God, *"After everything I've been through . . . why me?"* I've heard people say that God won't give you anything you can't handle, but I am here to tell you, that just isn't true.

I had spent my whole life fighting to see, and now my dad reached down and grabbed me by my shoulders. This wasn't the first time I had been faced with unbelievable adversity. I thought of all I'd been through and what I'd learned as a child about achieving my dreams. As my dad helped me to my feet, I wondered how I could ever find another dream. Maybe I didn't even want to dream again. But deep inside, I knew that whatever happened next, it would start with the people in that room. It would begin with my family.

CHAPTER 2

FAMILY FOREVER

Everything good in my life has started with my family. My faith, my positivity, my love for people, my thankfulness, and my drive to go after my dream are all things that have grown out of my having such a strong family.

I learned early on that my definition of family was a little bit different from other people's. To me, "family" doesn't just mean the people who are related to me by blood. Families are the people who are there for each other during the good times and during the bad. When I use the word "family," I mean the people in my life who choose to show up for one another. This has kept me level and surrounded by good people my whole life. It has also helped me stay away from people who aren't about the right things. Family has made me who I am today. That Saturday night in June at Aunt Evelyn's house, when I looked around the room, I didn't just see coaches, pastors, friends, and teachers . . . I saw my family.

Every dream has obstacles. My first big challenge was that my biological father wasn't around when I was little. The man who helped me to my feet in Aunt Evelyn's house, and had done so many times throughout my life, is Ben Green, my stepdad. Ben has always been and will always be my dad. He was there for me when my biological father wasn't. I don't say that with any anger in my heart or any bad feelings toward anyone. I have a good relationship now with my biological father—we talk from time to time and things between us are pretty good. People tell me that I got my size and athletic ability from him. He played basketball and is still heavily involved in coaching. His brother, my uncle Ike, had a solid professional basketball career; Ike played for a lot of different teams and was a really good post player. They have both been really helpful to me at times in my basketball career. But I could never have achieved my dreams on the basketball court without Ben in my life. He was there for me each and every step of the way. He was the guy who took me to practices, rebounded for me, helped me with my homework, stood by my side through the really tough moments, taught me about life, and showed me how to be a man. When I think about the people I admire and want to model my own life after, the first guy on my list is Ben Green, my dad.

So my story starts where my family really began, in Fresno, California, when my mom met Ben. He had been on the track team for a year at Baylor University, but then later he felt home-sick for California and returned to attend Fresno State, where he completed his college education. He was a fast athlete and was still doing some competitive running when he and my mom first started dating. I was only three years old when they met in 1997, and Ben tells me that when he saw me he swore that I had to be at least seven years old because I was so tall for my age.

One of their favorite things to do when they were dating, and one of my first memories of Ben, was to take me for bike rides at the park. Because of my size, they could never quite find a kid's bike that was big enough to fit me. (At four years old, I could al-ready fit into my mom's shoe size!) Dad says they would ride along the sidewalks at the park and he would laugh at the sight of me trying to pedal fast enough to keep up with him and Mom on a bike that was made for average-height kids.

I don't remember ever really missing my biological dad when I was young. Mom has told me that as her and Ben's wedding got closer, I would ask all the time if it would be okay for me to start calling him Dad. In fact, after I got to Baylor, I had "Green" tattooed on my arm to honor him and am hoping to someday change my last name legally to Austin-Green so that everyone knows what an important part he's played in my life. From the time I can remember anything about my childhood in California, Ben was there . . . showing up in my life, picking me up when I needed it. So his being the one to reach down and pick me up off the floor that terrible night of June 21 was nothing new.

Fresno was a beautiful place to live. The weather was always perfect and Mom and Dad moved into a house on a cul-de-sac right next door to the Drati family. Ben Drati was Dad's best friend from Fresno State; he had played football there and was the principal at Clovis West High School, where Dad also worked as a student adviser. Dad would mediate when students had fights with teachers or other students, help them resolve arguments, and counsel them when they had scheduling problems. If you've ever met Ben, you'd know this was the perfect job for him. He's really good at talking with people and helping them work out their problems. He's even-keeled and doesn't get upset easily.

Even on weeknights our house was always full of kids. We had a swimming pool in the backyard, and all through my elementary school years, swimming was one of my favorite things to do. I went to Fort Washington Elementary, and it was close enough to ride my bike to and from school each day with my friend Clayton. It was one of those neighborhoods where everyone knows each other pretty well and you really didn't even need to lock your doors at night. It was a perfect community for kids.

I began to learn how important family is and how the word "family" doesn't just mean the people you are related to by blood. We spent so much of our time with the Dratis that we became like one big family, and we are still very close with them today and visit them sometimes in California. We would eat dinners together, go to ball games, to the park, and to church—it seemed like we were always hanging out. At the end of the day, especially when my little brother and sister came along, the close relationship with the Dratis taught me a lot about responsibility. Their daughter Shaneece was my age and a good friend of mine, so we basically took care of each other's little brothers and sisters like they were our own. This is why, even today, I am so comfortable working around kids at camps and at Mo's Academy. My buddies would come over in grade school and I remember not understanding how in the world they could not know how to change a diaper! Changing diapers was just a routine part of life for me and Shaneece.

I don't know what she was thinking, but my mom let me have a pet snake, and each Friday night we would go buy a mouse to feed to the snake. Our dads would be across the street working at the high school football game, and so our two families of kids would gather around as the snake ate the mouse for dinner. The funniest thing was that no matter how many times Shaneece watched us feeding that snake, she would still always scream. While we kids fought like brothers and sisters, I don't think our moms and dads ever really argued with each other. But no matter what, we had each other's backs. As kids, we thought it was very cool that our dads, Ben and Ben, worked at the high school football field that was across the street from our homes. The actual Clovis West High School, located farther away from the field, was within walking distance of our elementary school.

I was a pretty good student in elementary school, but it could still be hard at times. It never really had anything to do with the actual schoolwork, though. Being tall like I am has its benefits, but it could be difficult to deal with, too. I was so much taller than everyone else in my grade that I would get called out in class for doing things that other boys would do just because I was easier to see than everyone else.

This was a big lesson and one that I am still figuring out sometimes. I am so tall that I get noticed no matter what. No matter where I go, even on the court, I can never be just part of the crowd. I always stand out. What was true in elementary school is still true for me today. I enjoy meeting new people and talking to them, but I can't just walk to class like a normal student without stopping to take a picture or getting caught up in a conversation with someone. Most days I love it, but I have to admit, sometimes it can wear me out to always have to be on my game and in a good mood. One day I walked into a class at Baylor and accidentally had my headphones on (like most of the other college students), but because I am seven feet tall and so noticeable, I was the one who got called out by the professor.

In elementary school, I was a pretty goofy and awkward kid. I was not just super tall, but I was also very skinny *and* I had to wear glasses. What kid wants to wear glasses? Dad tells me that I would try to sink down in my chair or bend over a little when I walked so that I wouldn't stand out from everybody else. It never worked, though. Everybody that age has something they don't like about themselves that they've got to work through: too skinny, too fat, too tall, too short, glasses, no glasses, or even feeling like your feet are too big. It seems funny when you get older and look back, but at the time it can be tough. It's just part of growing up. You *never* "grow out" of being a foot taller than everyone, so I had to grow into being comfortable with it.

I remember getting in trouble one time at Fort Washington. Mom and Dad were always so concerned about my education that Dad came over to observe me in class one day. He noticed that I moved around a lot in my seat, but because I was so big, it stood out more to the teacher. I don't know about you, but getting in trouble at school was never tolerated in my house. This is when Dad started teaching me that I needed to hold myself to a higher standard than other kids. Because of my height, people expected me to be more mature, so that's how I needed to act.

One thing I've always been able to do well is hear people and remember what they said the first time, or see something just once and remember it clearly. I don't know if I have a photographic memory or anything like that, but I never had to study really hard. My grades were always good, especially in math and science.

I HONESTLY CAN'T remember a time in my life without basketball, but my parents will tell you it all began with the competitive youth basketball program called Little Hoopsters held at Clovis West High School. This is where my love of basketball began and the dream of playing professionally was planted in my heart. My mom and dad signed me up when I was four years old, even though you had to be at least five to play. I was so tall that no one asked any questions. No matter when or where I played as a kid, it always seemed like I was the tallest guy on the court.

At that very young age, I would dribble a ball around the house all the time, even though Mom would get onto me about it. And when she chased me out of the living room or kitchen, I would go into the bathroom, lock the door, and dribble for hours on the tile floor. There was never a day when I didn't play ball or work on my game. When I had a ball in my hands, it seemed to help me focus. It made me happy. I could just dribble, play, and shoot for hours on end without even thinking about the time.

When I was in elementary school, my favorite player was Allen Iverson. Whenever he was on television, I was watching. I loved how he dribbled the ball and how he always played so hard. The funny thing is, I wasn't super coordinated when I wasn't on the court playing basketball, but when I had the ball in my hands I was always trying to do something with it that I saw Iverson do on television. Perhaps that's one of the reasons that I developed the ball-handling skills I have today. Mom and Dad say that during my very first Little Hoopsters game as a four-year-old, I got the ball from the inbounds pass and started dribbling it up the court between my legs, which very few kids in my league could do even though they were much older.

I tried to play some other sports when I was in elementary and even middle school. I was a really good golfer (I still am). I liked baseball a lot and was a solid pitcher. Being tall and lanky gave me an advantage on the mound, and I could throw a baseball pretty hard for my age. But basketball was definitely my thing. I know, as a kid, I watched the NBA draft on the television in our house. And from the time I was little, I could just see myself walking across the stage on NBA draft night. That's the best way that I can explain it. It wasn't like one night I just had a dream about it and it stuck with me. Mom and Dad definitely didn't talk about it. They were always more concerned with how I behaved and how I did in school. My dream was there as soon as I started to play ball, but what kid doesn't dream of playing in the NBA?

But it wasn't just wishful thinking for me—I knew it was going to happen someday.

I played in the Little Hoopsters program all through elementary school. I kept getting taller and I would work every day on handling the ball and shooting. At first, when I was out there playing games, I wanted to have the ball in my hands at all times. From the very moment I first stepped on the court, I was a perfectionist. That's why I practiced for hours every day, never thinking about the time. And when I stepped on the court, I absolutely couldn't tolerate losing. For some kids, always having the ball works out because they aren't a foot taller than everyone else. But my coaches always wanted me to get close to the basket, to shoot and rebound in the paint. I wasn't having any of that. I wanted to show off my Allen Iverson moves! I wanted to dribble it up the court and shoot the ball myself every single time because I was so competitive. Mom and Dad were always there, yelling at me from the stands, "Pass the ball, Isaiah!" or "Get in the paint, Isaiah." I guess after a couple of years of hearing that, I finally gave in and started to listen to them. I owe my mom and dad all the credit for teaching me to be an unselfish player.

Dad will be the first to tell you he isn't a basketball guy, but he did everything he could to help me become a better player. In fact, as much as it was up to him, I don't think he ever missed a game. One of the big ways he helped was by always working to get me around really good coaches. One time, Dad and I were shooting ball on the neighborhood court we had set up on the cul-de-sac. (I think sixth grade was the last time he could take me in a game of one-on-one.) I'm not joking when I say that there were always at least ten kids hanging around our house to play ball. There was always a game going on out there after school, so this was probably a Saturday morning. Dad was trying to teach me a new move. He said, "Isaiah, what you really need to add to your game is a skyhook. Because you're so tall out there, if you can shoot a skyhook, nobody will be able to block it." I laughed at him and said that there was no way I was going to shoot a sky-hook. I shook my head and told him the skyhook was an old-man shot. But a couple of weeks later I was playing with all the best players in the area on an AAU (Amateur Athletic Union) team when it actually happened. I caught the ball in the paint and before I knew it, I was shooting Dad's favorite shot—the skyhook. To this day, I think he believes that shot is what turned me into an elite-level basketball player. I don't even try to argue with him about that anymore—I just have to laugh.

THERE WERE ALSO some tough times when I was young. Since I had always been a good pitcher, that summer Mom and Dad thought that I should go over to the high school for a baseball camp that was being put on by the varsity coaches and players. They were always getting me into camps during the summers because they didn't want me hanging around the house with nothing to do. That summer, my basketball practices and games were at night, so they sent me to Clovis High School during the day for the weeklong baseball clinic.

I was already over six feet tall as a sixth grader, so when I went out for camp some of the coaches wanted to put me in the group with the older kids. I told them I didn't want to, but I didn't want to be disrespectful to the coaches. I had played a lot of rec-league baseball, but never on very competitive teams. I was playing first base that afternoon with kids four or five years older than me. Being so young, I never realized that the pitcher, in the middle of facing a batter, might turn and throw the ball to me at first base. Sure enough, halfway through a scrimmage, he came out of his stance very quickly and threw the ball in my direction, trying to keep the runner at first from taking too big of a lead and stealing a base. I was watching the batter's box and not paying attention, so I didn't see the ball until the very last second, but it was too late; I wasn't able to get my glove up in time to stop it. The ball hit me directly in my right eye so hard that I fell backward, crying in pain.

All of the coaches sprinted over to check on me. Dad's friend coached the team, and he had already called him to pick me up and take me to the hospital. He and Mom had been out running errands that day with my little brother and sister. My eye began to swell up so big that I couldn't see anything at all. I had just started wearing contacts that year, and the force of the pitch was so hard that my eye was swollen shut for almost a week before the doctor and my mom could pry my eye open enough to get my contact out.

My injury was so bad—my face swollen and vision so poor—that I didn't get to play in a junior Olympics basketball tournament for my first real AAU team. Missing any kind of basketball felt like a punishment for me. It was terrible to know that my team was playing and I couldn't be out there with them.

The doctors told my parents some interesting things about my eyes. They said that because of their size and shape, it forced my retinas to be pulled abnormally tight. They warned us that because of the severity of the baseball injury, if I was ever hit in the right eye again it could completely detach my retina and leave me with permanent damage to my vision. It was really hard to sit out of basketball, but for the most part, my life went on and I didn't think about my eyes. I was just being a kid again—swimming at the house, playing golf, and practicing basketball all the time. I even played my first season of football that year and caught a pass for a touchdown. But I never, ever wanted to play another inning of baseball after my accident.

THAT YEAR, MOM got a job offer, but it meant moving to Atlanta in the spring. After she and Dad talked about it, they decided to stay in California. She regretted not taking that big promotion, and Dad told her that if something else came along she should definitely take the job. That summer, something else did come along. She was offered another chance at a promotion, but only if we would be willing to move to Minnesota.

I remember when they sat down to tell me the news. I was pretty upset. I didn't know anything about Minnesota except that it snowed a whole lot there. I had the perfect life in Fresno. Even when I was in the sixth grade, the varsity basketball coaches at Clovis West High School knew me by name and were excited about having me play in their program. I liked the coaches and so did Dad. We also lived right next door to the Dratis, who had become part of our family. They were our best friends in the whole world. I took the news pretty hard and really couldn't understand why they would even think about moving. Dad really helped me, though, by sitting me down and explaining that sometimes in life you have to leave what feels comfortable in order to find success.

After my sophomore year in college, when I was trying to decide if I should declare for the NBA draft, I thought about the conversation we had that day in Fresno about moving. Baylor was my home, and it felt comfortable to be there around my guys and the coaches who had become part of my family. I had my family in Waco and it began to feel like Fresno once had for me. I thought a lot about how my parents handled the Minnesota opportunity and what Dad said about finding success. Sometimes if you want to pursue your dream, you have to be willing to leave a good situation behind for the unknown. It was a great lesson that I've never forgotten.

That winter, the year before I was about to go to middle school, we packed up our house in Fresno and moved all the way across the country to Minnesota. We made the move in January, and when we got to Minnesota there was already a foot or more of snow on the ground. It was quite a shock coming from sunny Fresno, where it never really got cold. I had never seen so much snow in my life. We moved to a town called Woodbury, near St. Paul, and I started to attend Lake Middle School. When my younger brother, Noah, and I began school it was pretty difficult, especially for him. He's an outgoing kid, but anytime you're the new kid it takes some adjusting. It was easier for me to make friends because I was already six foot four, so people at school would want to come up and talk to me. As the biggest guy at school, I was always asked how tall I was or people would want to know my shoe size. In the sixth grade I could already wear my dad's shoes, and even then, they were kind of tight.

Mom and Dad say that the move was hard for them, too. They had trouble getting adjusted to being away from everything they had known in Fresno. I'm not going to lie; Minnesota was the coldest place I had ever been. It was the biggest change I had ever been through up to that point in my life, and that spring seemed really long. But being in a new place and not really knowing anyone actually forced us to be together and rely on each other more. The move was difficult, but it taught us that no matter what, we still had each other. Noah, Narah, and I wouldn't be as close as we are today without that time in our lives.

Looking back, I can see how much Ben becoming my dad meant to me as a kid and can see more clearly how much my childhood helped me understand the real meaning of family. My dream started with my family, who taught me to be thankful and to focus on what I have instead of what I don't have. Being thankful gave me the energy and positivity to go after my dreams. I'll always be grateful for my time in Fresno and the friendship of the Drati family. There was a strong foundation being built during that time that I would have to lean on as an adult.

THE TEARS ROLLED down my face as I sat on the floor of my aunt and uncle's house in Dallas on June 21, 2014, just days before the NBA draft, and as my dad, the guy who had been there for me my whole life, slowly helped me up, there was a voice in the back of my mind that calmed me. My family taught me to be thankful for what I have instead of focusing on what I don't have, and that room was full of family and support.

CHAPTER 3

I BELONG

You can't make your dreams a reality until you learn to believe in yourself, until you find that moment when you are convinced that you belong. Dad's words about sometimes having to move out of a place you feel comfortable to find success turned out to be true, but not without some adversity. Our move was difficult, but everything turned out okay once we were settled in Minnesota.

As I entered my junior high years, I began to learn how to

handle myself on the court, and then I really started to understand that my dream could come true. I had always believed it, but in the next few years I would begin to see that I actually belonged in my dream. When I began playing in junior high, my competitive spirit started to grow along with my height. I had always been able to win on the basketball court, but now my drive to succeed became a passion.

Mom and Dad started marking our heights on a doorway in the kitchen, and just a couple of months after we moved into our new house in Minnesota, I hit six feet four inches. It was only the spring of my seventh-grade year. That was my toughest year in school, because I was growing so fast that I could never quite find clothes that fit me.

My frustration with how big I was had started the month before we moved from California. All of the kids at my school in Fresno were wearing shoes with special wheels that could pop out from the bottom when you wanted to skate around on them. One of the popular singers at the time would wear them and skate all over the stage. It is funny to think about it now, but I wanted a pair of those shoes so bad. There was just one problem: my feet had grown so big that I was wearing adult-size shoes, and those skate shoes only came in kids' sizes. So not only did I stick out among my friends because of my height, but I didn't fit in because I couldn't wear these cool shoes. When you're that age, fitting in is a pretty big deal.

In Minnesota, my growth continued to cause some more awkwardness for me. My parents couldn't find pants that would fit me. Roller-skate shoes are one thing, but pants are essential. I was way too tall for kids' sizes but way too skinny to fit into men's sizes. My parents would buy really nice jeans and cut them just below the knee so they were like long shorts on me. I didn't mind being tall so much at this point, but I was very self-conscious about being skinny. Sometimes I would even take Ben's shirts from his closet and wear them to school because I thought they might make me look bigger. I thought they would hide how skinny I actually was, but looking back at pictures, I see that it didn't work out as well as I had thought.

Although my height made me feel awkward at school, it helped me on the court. I still wasn't excited about playing in the paint, but my height and athleticism made me a tough guard for anyone my age. I played on the junior high team at Lake Middle School. We didn't lose many games. I was getting noticed as a player around the city because I never came across anyone who could successfully guard me. I was learning how to take over a game and make my teammates better as well.

My game was challenged when I began playing for Coach Shaun Tillman and the 43 Hoops AAU team. My height guaranteed me a spot on the team. We were *really* good. Coach Tillman was the first coach I had who pushed me to keep my emotions in check on the floor. My competitive nature was growing, and the best way I can explain it is that I couldn't tolerate losing or messing up. This kind of behavior had started before we moved to Minnesota, when I was playing Little Hoopsters in California, but as I faced tougher competition, I became more and more determined to win. There was one game when Dad's friend Kevin was officiating, and he made such a bad call that I lost my cool with him. I was walking down the court upset about the call, and I could see that my parents were disappointed at my reaction. I was angry at how his bad call had cost my team, but I didn't realize that my reaction was probably also hurting my team.

I started to play with an edge on the court, almost mad sometimes. Most of the time this worked to my advantage, but if I got a bad call or made the wrong play, my temper could get a little out of control. It was like all of a sudden I would start seeing red out there on the court. I was easygoing and quiet off the court, but when I was playing, I expected to do well and I required my teammates to do the same. If that didn't happen, I didn't mind telling whoever wasn't doing their job all about it.

Coaches love when you play harder and with more passion than anyone else on the court, but when it turns to anger, that's not a good thing—for you or your team.

Coach Tillman was a good Christian leader who was always focused on developing his players as young men. He wouldn't tolerate me getting mad while I was playing. He would sit me on the bench and tell me I wasn't going back in the game until I got my mind right. Looking back, I know this is a tough thing for a coach to do with one of his best players, because sometimes it means you might lose the game, but he did it anyway.

Mom wasn't shy about sitting me out either, but for her own reasons. She wanted to make sure there was never a doubt in my mind about what was most important to her. She discovered one day that I had received a D on a test the weekend before an important tournament. Grades were always more important than any basketball game to Mom. She called Coach Tillman and told him that I would be there on the bench to support my team, but I wasn't allowed to play.

Believe me, it was one of the last times I ever got a D on a test.

Minnesota had a different level of competition than I had played in California. There were a lot of things I had to learn. I remember being shocked when people (yes, adults) would heckle me from the stands. One time during a game, a guy in the crowd was on me so bad that I went over to Dad and asked him if he could make him be quiet. I had to learn at a young age to block out the fans and anything else that was happening except for the game. It was a good lesson about focusing on what was right in front of me on the court and ignoring distractions—a lesson most players have to learn to be successful.

I always respected Coach Tillman because I knew his expectations, and they were always clear. He was always consistent, always fair, always trying to make me a better basketball player and a better man. The basketball court became the one place where I didn't feel awkward at all. It became the one place, other than with my family, where I started to believe I belonged. It was my home away from home.

We won the state AAU title that year and I earned my first championship ring. Then we went on to Iowa and won the regional AAU championship.

Things were starting to look up for my basketball dreams, but there was a moment in Minnesota that would come back to haunt me. When I went to the doctor for some routine tests, medical professionals thought they detected an irregular heartbeat. Mom and Dad were worried about the discovery and so we went back for more testing. The doctors couldn't quite figure out what was going on with me and wanted to make sure that I was healthy enough to play basketball. The doctors told my parents that one of the many possibilities was this disease we had never heard of called Marfan syndrome. The problem with their theory, though, was that I had no family history of the disease. I had never shown any of the physical symptoms of the syndrome or any other heart issues when I was out there playing on the court. The whole thing seemed to just come out of the blue, but we were convinced that I was fine. Still, the doctors ran some tests just to be sure, and we were happy when the results came back negative. They didn't find any evidence of my having the disease.

I was cleared to keep playing basketball. It seemed like the whole medical ordeal was just a bump in the road.

I WAS IN the seventh grade when I began to get letters from colleges. I'll never forget that first one. It wasn't just any college; it was a recruiting letter from UCLA. Dad started naming off the big men who had played there, like Hall of Famers Kareem Abdul-Jabbar and Bill Walton, and even current NBA star Kevin Love. I came home from school that day to a lot of excitement as my parents and I read that letter of interest from a powerhouse basketball program. It was a very big deal. My parents still have that first letter.

The greatest thing was that the letters kept coming in. More and more colleges began showing interest in me as a seventh grader. Of course, Mom and Dad were more focused on me getting a college education than they ever were about basketball, but I started to believe that my dream was actually going to become a reality. At that age, I would hear a lot of the other kids in school talk about wanting to play professionally, but most knew it was wishful thinking. But I could see my hopes and dreams coming true with each mail delivery. I noticed that when I talked about the NBA, other people would take it seriously. Even Mom started to take it seriously, but she would always make sure to follow up with a comment about the importance of getting my education first.

Things started changing fast for me when I was invited to an elite AAU camp the summer after seventh grade. It was an Adidas camp in Ohio, and all of the best players in the country were invited. Guys like L. J. Rose, Rasheed Sulaimon, Marcus Smart, and Phil Forte. There were a lot of tall kids at that camp, but no one was as tall as me. At that point I had grown closer to six-seven, but I couldn't have weighed much more than a buck ten. I could pass, shoot, and block shots, but I still wasn't that good at rebounding or playing physical in the lane. Dad couldn't get to the first day of games because he was finishing up some work; it is one of the only times I can ever remember him missing one of my games when I was a kid. When he got to the camp, I was so excited. I had played a great game that first night. I couldn't wait to tell him that I had even scored twenty points!

The next day, the games didn't go nearly as well for me. I was pushed around a lot and came off the floor feeling pretty bad about how poorly I played. Dad had a talk with me about taking my game to the next level. If it was going to happen, he thought I needed to become a more physical player. It wasn't that I didn't try to be physical on the court. I was just so light that I could easily be pushed around. It didn't matter how much I ate or what I did, I never could keep weight on. I was going to try to play more physical, but the truth is that once I arrived at camp I started to get a little bit scared. I knew I was good, but I was struggling to believe that I belonged on the court with such elite players.

At the end of the second day, they handed out invites to the top guys for the final game of the camp. It was like the All-Star game of the All-Star camp. Only a handful of the best players were asked to participate. Right in the middle of doubting myself, I was shocked to get an invite to play in the game. A lot of the other campers probably thought I didn't deserve to be invited.

If there is a moment I can point to during those years that really helped me believe I could accomplish my dream, it would be receiving that invitation. Here I was with the greatest players in the country, and I had been placed in the starting lineup of the All-Star game. Those coaches may have picked me because of my potential, but it didn't matter—I was determined to prove myself out there. That game was a turning point for me. I was still a little bit nervous when I got out on the floor, but I focused on what Dad and I had talked about. I tried to play in the lane. The game was intense, but I rose to the occasion. I blocked shots . . . and *rebounded*! Dad later told me that that All-Star game was the moment when he thought to himself that I had the potential to be an elite player.

WE LIVED IN Minnesota for less than two years and were still getting adjusted when Mom received another promotion. This time we were going to Texas. We flew down to visit a couple of times, but we were moving during AAU season. Since I was already getting recruited from colleges all over the country, it was important for me to find a good team to play for in Texas. That's when my parents met Coach Rick Roberts. He became friends with my mom and dad and helped them get to know the Dallas area. I started traveling the country playing for his team before we actually moved into our new house in Dallas.

It was a great team. There were some unbelievable athletes on that squad. Ricky Roberts was the coach's son and was a great guard who went on to play at Central Oklahoma. Marcus Smart and Phil Forte ended up at Oklahoma State, Je'lon Hornbeak went to Oklahoma, and Johnathan Gray was one the best running backs in the country and eventually played football for the Texas Longhorns. Those guys accepted me with open arms and ended up being some of my closest friends. We were called Team Texas, and Coach Roberts had us playing against the best competition in America.

Coach Rick was an awesome mentor and coach. He wouldn't discourage me from doing some of the things on the floor that showcased my skills as a big guy. He let me play on the perimeter and bring the ball up, but he made his expectations for me clear.

He would tell me how many rebounds and blocked shots he needed from me in each summer game, and if I met his goals, then he would let me do what I wanted to do with the ball during the game. My temper could still be a little negative on the court, but our team was so good and the players got along so well that it didn't come up much. Coach Roberts was the same as Coach Tillman, though; he didn't tolerate any outbursts on the court. If I had a problem during the game, he would sit me down next to him on the bench until I was able to calm down and refocus.

We ended up moving to Mansfield in the Dallas area, since it was considered a great school district. Ben had been working at one of the Woodbury schools when we lived in Minnesota, but with another move and Mom traveling for work, he decided to stay home and help Noah, Narah, and me get adjusted. By the time I walked through the doors of Worley Middle School my eighth-grade year, I was just over six feet eight inches tall. I had visited other states across the country for games and played against the best players in the nation and was more than holding my own. By then I was getting so many letters from different colleges that some days our mailbox was literally filled to the top. It was crazy.

I met Coach Mills and Coach Dwon Clifton (who would later become my agent) and some of the other coaches from Baylor that year. Coach Roberts knew everyone in Texas basketball, and he introduced me to many of those people. Baylor started showing interest in me during my eighth-grade year; they had watched me in some summer tournament games. Since my dad had run track at Baylor, he enjoyed taking me down to Waco to visit the campus. I will never forget going to basketball games there as a kid and getting to go back into the coach's offices and meet Coach Drew afterward. He was one of my favorite people. But I wasn't really interested in choosing a college. My parents wanted to expose me to Baylor because it was the largest Christian university in the country and also a great academic school. I just loved basketball and thought it was cool to go to the home games in Waco.

My junior high team hadn't been too successful before I started. At the beginning of my season there, I wanted to make a mark. Ricky Roberts and I were both on the team; we played great together and knew how to win, so I was sure we would win a title. I remember standing around in the locker room before the first practice, and I told our coach that we were going to win the championship. He just looked at me and shook his head. But I was confident we would be there.

We played in a competitive conference, and some of the guys on my AAU team played for other eighth-grade squads around the Metroplex. We had some battles, but we never lost. I was continuing to grow and becoming a more complete player on the court, especially as a post player. Still light for my size, I was becoming a dominant shot blocker and rebounder. Ricky was our point guard and we worked well together on the court. We ran through the season and the post-season tournament all the way up to the championship game. We were going to play our school's biggest rival in the city final. Ricky and I were hyped because our Team Texas teammate Je'lon Hornbeak played for the other team. This game was significant all by itself, but it would also mean bragging rights when we got to AAU practice.

And I was hoping for another championship.

THE GYM WAS completely packed and excited that night for the game. Dad sat with Coach Roberts in the stands and watched warm-ups. My adrenaline was flowing, and I was flying around the court a hundred miles an hour. I remember the first time through the layup line I went up and dunked it. I could dunk the ball pretty easily back then, but I hadn't ever thrown it down hard. Somewhere in between that first dunk during warm-ups and me coming back up to the front of the line, the referees must've arrived in the gym. In basketball, once the officials come in and blow the whistle during pregame, you are no longer allowed to dunk. I was so focused on getting ready for the game that I didn't hear the whistle or realize that the refs had come out on the floor.

I took the ball in the layup line and drove to the basket. I don't know exactly why it all happened in that moment. I felt like

I wanted to tear the rim down. I went up and dunked the ball harder than I ever had in my life. It was a great feeling. I remember it even rocked the backboard. I knew it was intimidating to the opposing team, because there was no one else on the court who could dunk like that. The crowd in the packed gym went wild. Dad says it was the first time he had seen me dunk with that kind of authority. He and Coach Roberts looked at each other and said how exciting it was to see me throw it down with that type of aggression. I was just hyped to win a championship.

The next thing I knew the whistle was blowing again; this time it was directed at me. I tried to explain to the officials that I hadn't heard the first whistle, but they didn't want to hear anything I had to say. They gave our team a technical foul and I was ejected from the game before my team even took the court. I had worked all year for the championship, and I wouldn't be able to play in the biggest game of the season. But being ejected wasn't the only bad result of that pregame disaster. Something else happened when I dunked that ball—something strange. When my feet hit the floor and I took my first step, all of a sudden I started seeing red. I'm not talking about being angry; the vision in my right eye was literally *red*. It didn't hurt, and it wasn't a terrible feeling. It was just obvious that something was wrong. I sat at the end of the bench more concerned about my team and the game we were playing than I was about my eye. But it was like someone had placed a red lens over my right eye.

I was the only six-eight kid playing for either team that night, so I knew I would have dominated. If I wouldn't have gotten thrown out, we could've won by a lot. But with me on the bench, it became a close game. Fortunately, Ricky Roberts took over and had an incredible night. We ended up doing just what I had predicted to Coach at the start of the season. We won the city championship. We had bragging rights over Je'lon, at least for a couple of months. I thought my parents would be upset with me about the pregame dunk, but they weren't. I'm not sure they thought it was fair that I was ejected from the game, and since they already knew how disappointed I was from being unable to play in the big game, not much was said about it during the ride home. I said nothing to them about my eye. We were busy talking about the game, and I was so excited about the win that it was all I could think about.

Once we got home, I was heading to take a shower when I stopped to tell my dad that I had dunked the ball so hard that I was seeing red. My parents both laughed about it, thinking I was joking and that I saw red because my dunk was that unbelievable. Later that evening, though, my vision really started to bother me. I had played two years of football and taken a few big hits, but I had never had anything like this happen with my eye before.

I waited a couple of hours, hoping that it would go back to normal on its own. I remember coming in and explaining to Mom and Dad that the vision in my right eye was completely red, and it seemed to be getting worse by the minute. As we began to talk about it, my parents quickly realized it was the same eye that I had injured a couple of years earlier in the baseball accident before we moved from California.

My parents were really concerned then, so they called the after-hours line at the local eye doctor. The doctor said he could see us immediately, even though it was pretty late in the evening. I had always worn glasses or contacts, and we had been to this doctor's office before; it was only a few miles from our house. When we got there and the doctor examined my eye, he looked concerned. He immediately referred me to an eye specialist in Dallas.

We went to the specialist the next morning and received terrible news—my retina was torn. Not just torn, but it was one of the worst retinal tears the doctor had ever seen. There was only one doctor qualified and willing to do the operation. I was going to lose my sight unless they could get me into emergency surgery to repair my eye. So many things had gone right for me in those early years. Just when I started to realize that I really belonged in my NBA dream, I was about to run into the biggest challenge of my life yet.

CHAPTER 4

MY EXCUSE OR MY STORY

I've heard my preachers talk about going from the mountain-top to the valley. I learned the meaning of that saying at a pretty young age, and it taught me something very important about life's obstacles. It's a lesson that would help push me closer to my dream of playing in the NBA and also help me find a way to get up off the foyer floor that night at my aunt Evelyn's house. I was about to go through some of the toughest times in my life. But my mom had always taught me that when life hits you with a situation that seems impossible, you are left with only two ways to really see it.

Gregory Kozielec, who is one of the best eye surgeons in the country, explained that my torn retina was one of the worst he had ever seen. I felt pretty calm, even in the face of emergency surgery, because the basketball season had already ended and I had some time off before AAU would start. Basketball was my only real concern, and in my mind, there was plenty of time for me to get back on my feet and ready to play. I just wanted to get through it and was hopeful that things would work out. In those minutes before I went into surgery, I couldn't have imagined what the road ahead of me would be like. The doctor told my parents he felt pretty good about being able to repair the damage. It was going to be a difficult process because repairs on people my age were intricate, and this was one of the most challenging retinal tears he had ever seen, but if I didn't go through with the operation there was no doubt I would quickly lose all the vision in my right eye.

The operation took place on February 12, 2008, in Dallas. It felt like it took all day, although I know the actual procedure was just a couple of hours long. The doctors went in with lasers and cut directly into my eye to reattach my retina. Then they put some type of oil into my eye to make sure that everything would heal correctly. When I did finally wake from surgery, Mom, Dad, Noah, and Narah were all there waiting to see me. My first thought as I awoke was that I was really thirsty. But my second thought was all about the pain. It was unbelievable pain. To this day, it is the most excruciating pain I've ever felt. The only way I can describe it is for you to imagine having a thousand long needles being stuck directly into your eye.

The first few moments after surgery were also the only time that I was allowed to sit upright for some time. The doctors immediately came in and had me turn over, and I would spend most of the next few weeks lying facedown so that my eye could heal correctly. They also sent me home with a pillow for my face, like the ones you see on massage tables, and a three-way mirror that I could lay under me on the floor so I could look around the room. The pain, especially in those first few days, continued to be unbearable, but Mom and Dad were there for me throughout the whole experience.

My mom keeps our family grounded. She lifts us all up when life isn't going well. At night, she came home to sit and pray over me, sometimes all night after a full day at work. I am not sure how she did it. The pain seemed to be worse at night, and the house was quiet so there was less to distract me from it. If you've ever had major surgery, you understand what pain meds do. The first few days I tried taking them, but they didn't really make the pain go away, but made me feel out of it. If there is one thing I can't stand, it's not being completely aware of everything that's going on. After a day or two, I decided that

I would rather deal with the full-on pain than lose track of my days, so I stopped taking the medicine.

Have you ever had something hurt so bad that you actually couldn't cry about it? That's how the first weeks of recovery felt. I tried to sleep as much as I possibly could. The only times I got up from lying facedown for two whole weeks were to eat or go to the bathroom. I stayed positive, though—this was just a bump in the road, and soon I would be back on my feet and in the gym. When you love something as much as I love basketball, it's miserable to not be able to shoot or dribble or play. The short time off and hearing people talk about the possibility of losing my sight made me realize that I should never take playing ball for granted. When I got back to the gym I was going to work even harder.

After two really long weeks, I was ready to return to the doctor for my checkup. I had been wearing a patch over my eye during the recovery, so I didn't think too much about it. I couldn't tell if my sight was getting better. I was, however, feeling ready to get on with my life—to get back to pursuing my dream. I had been texting with my Team Texas guys and was hoping I would be cleared to get out on the court.

I went into the checkup feeling positive. I had survived the worst of it. I would get checked out and then be back on the court playing with my guys.

But the checkup didn't go quite the way I had imagined.

When Dr. Kozielec came in to talk with me and my family, he gave us some very bad news. There was way too much scar tissue building up around my eye. If it was left alone, my retina was not going to heal correctly.

He said that I was going to need another operation.

I had just barely made it through the worst pain I had ever experienced, so it was very difficult to learn that I had to go through it all over again. This was also tough because another surgery was going to keep me off the court even longer and cut into the AAU basketball season.

The second surgery, on March 6, was every bit as hard as the first; the recovery was just as painful. I've never hated school, but I've never really loved it either, and it was the first time in my life I actually started to miss being in class. I would have much rather sat through a million English classes than lie facedown in so much pain.

THROUGH IT ALL, Dad was there for me every day. He made sandwiches for me, helped with meds, picked me up, and kept me strong when I would get discouraged. Some of my teammates, like Ricky, Je'lon, Phil, and Marcus, came by the house to check in on me. I wasn't allowed to play video games or watch television because the doctors didn't want to stimulate my eye during recovery, so the time passed by very slowly. The first few nights were tough.

After the second surgery, when my mom wasn't traveling for work and I was unable to sleep because of the pain, she would come in my room and sit with me at night to talk. One of those evenings, something strange and wonderful happened that changed the way I saw my life and my future.

My parents had always taken us to church. Like a lot of kids my age, I would always tell people that I believed in God. But other than going to church with my parents or listening to them talk about the Bible, it didn't mean much to me. I liked church and enjoyed the Bible stories I heard there. I prayed when I was asked to at dinner and stuff like that, but I didn't make a practice of talking to God on my own or even of reading the Bible.

But that night Mom was praying over me like she had done so often—she may even have thought I had gone to sleep. I couldn't go anywhere and didn't have any distractions, so I began to focus on her prayer. Mom could really say some intense prayers when we needed her to, and during my recoveries she was often in my room, putting her hand on my shoulder and asking God to heal me and to help me get through the pain and frustration. They were good prayers—I really was dealing with a lot of pain and frustration!

But this night was different.

It was one of those times you just can't explain other than to say that God came into my room while Mom was praying over me. I thought about everything my parents believed and what an important part of my family life our faith had always seemed to be. I realized during that prayer that God was the reason my mom had her positive outlook on life. God was the reason my parents treated people the way they did. God was the reason I had all my talents and abilities. God seemed really close, even in the pain.

I closed my eyes and started to say my own prayer. I don't remember all that I prayed about that night. I know I told God that I wasn't sure why I had to go through the surgeries, but I was going to commit my life to Him. It was an emotional moment. I do remember praying that whatever God wanted or needed me to do, I would be willing to do it. People often talk about the moment when they are saved—that night with Mom praying over me, that was my moment. I just knew I belonged. My dream was no longer just mine. I was giving it back to God.

That's when I really made a serious commitment and began reading my Bible and praying all the time. Of course it was more than that, though. God loved people and that meant I needed to do the same. That's something Mom would always tell me. And I believe it—enough to even tattoo it on my arm. Through my family, I was building the foundation of my faith.

When I told Mom about my prayer, she taught me another lesson about having faith in God. She said, "Isaiah, the belief part is easy. Trusting in God's plan for you is where the real journey begins." I felt like I was ready to trust.

From that point on, my relationship with God became a huge part of my life. I have several of the Bible verses I love inked on my body so that I can always be reminded of what is most important in my life. That moment with Mom praying over me was life-changing. Whatever was happening in my life, God had a greater plan—one much bigger than playing in the NBA, whether that still happened or not. I felt like the more I read the Bible, the more I found out it was full of stories about people going through adversity but keeping faith that God was doing something good behind the scenes. And the Bible stories all show that God *is* working behind the scenes.

It felt like the story of my man Joseph in Genesis 39, when he gets thrown into prison. It seems so unfair, what happens to him. He is working for the king of Egypt, the Pharaoh. Joseph is a really loyal guy who is working hard and faithfully doing his job each day when the Pharaoh's wife spreads lies about him. The Pharaoh gets angry and commands that Joseph be locked away (even though he is completely innocent). That is some serious adversity! Joseph is probably thinking, "What did I do to deserve this?" But he still kept on trusting God. I guess I approached it like this torn retina was my adversity that I didn't quite deserve. But I began to trust that God was doing things maybe I couldn't see—maybe none of us could see. Faith takes work, just like basketball. Sometimes you can be in the zone, and other times, having faith means showing up and grinding it out. My faith soon became a real source of strength in my life. My faith would eventually help me choose my college, stay strong through so many difficult moments, understand the blessings in my life when things were going well, and it would play an important role in introducing me to many of the people that I call family.

I was still learning to trust, though—which was about to get pretty tough.

THE MOST DIFFICULT thing about this part of my story, besides the physical pain and having to sit out from the sport I loved, was the fact that every time I went through a surgery I was hopeful that my vision would be fixed. And after the second surgery, everything seemed to be good . . . at least for a couple of weeks. The recovery had been just as rough, but once I took the eye patch off and got back to playing ball, I found life with only one good eye was difficult. My right eye wasn't healed and my vision still wasn't completely the same.

That spring I went out to play with Team Texas to test the waters. I'll never forget my first practice. I was *really bad*. Those weeks were a huge challenge for me on the court. Jump shots that I would normally make? Air balls. I couldn't see the ball clearly when my teammates passed it to me because my depth perception was off. I had a hard time locating the ball to grab a rebound off the glass or block a shot. I was having trouble navigating my way up the floor on fast breaks or seeing guys move in the offense. It was scary how difficult playing could be with limited vision. It made me pray even more that my eye would heal. I just kept on trusting God that He would fix the problems with my eye and I kept hoping things would get better.

I was able to get some of my vision back. It was slow, and it was never quite clear. You know that feeling when you walk out of an air-conditioned building with your sunglasses on and they fog up quickly because it's so hot outside? That is what the vision in my right eye was like.

I was able to play a little bit and returned to school for a couple of weeks. Life seemed to be slowly getting back to normal, until June, when we went for another checkup. After Dr. Kozielec examined me, he said that I would need yet another surgery, this time to place a corrective lens over my right eye. I couldn't believe it. A third surgery! The operation was scheduled for June 10, and that meant there would be no AAU season for me that summer. I was getting recruited from all over the country and I wouldn't be able to play ball in a single tournament.

I had a lot of questions for God during that time. I was frustrated because I had kept praying for my sight to get better—we all kept praying for it to get better. I can't tell you how often during that time I thought about trust. Trusting God was the real work. My vision was still clear about playing in the NBA—it was just difficult for me to see from my right eye. It was also difficult to see where God was in all of this mess. He hadn't been answering my prayers. I was frustrated and confused about what He was doing in my life.

Dr. Kozielec is one of the top eye doctors in the country, so we trusted in his expertise. But we didn't really have any other options. Because my surgeries were so difficult, he was one of the few specialists willing to perform them. This would be my third surgery in just four short months. In this third operation, they inserted a lens over my eye. The lens was designed to clear up my vision. This seemed to be the last piece in the puzzle.

After the surgery, they asked me to stay immobilized for even longer. It was summer, during the AAU season, and I was unforgettably miserable. Still, I kept praying that *this* surgery would be the one to work. It was the kind of prayer where I was begging God for help. The whole process was so hard and I really didn't have time to get adjusted to seeing with one eye. But I stayed thankful. I was working to trust God. I kept my hopes up.

Through this whole trial my family kept quiet about the surgeries. My closest friends, my Team Texas guys, and our pastor, Ronnie Goines from Koinonia Church, were really the only people who knew about everything I was going through. Pastor Goines would pray over me whenever we would go to Sunday-morning service, and he would always take time to come and talk to me afterward. He encouraged me. I always walked away from our talks feeling like my faith had been strengthened. Mom and Dad weren't necessarily hiding the eye problems from people; we were just trusting that it would be corrected and that my vision would go back to normal. As college letters continued to pour into the mailbox, we didn't want to make a big story out of something that would eventually be fixed. Several weeks after the third surgery, I began to see a little more clearly out of my right eye. It felt like a miracle. The lens was working! I was getting ready to start my high school career and God had returned my vision.

SINCE I HAD missed the entire AAU season that summer, when fall rolled around I was ready to get into the gym for my freshman season. My first days of high school were pretty great. Mom and Dad kept a routine of doing a grade check every Friday night for all three of us kids, so I was on top of things at school. *My* dream was to play in the NBA, but Mom will be the first to tell you that *her* dream was for me to earn good grades and get a college education that would benefit me for my whole life.

Basketball started that year, and I had grown even taller, to nearly six foot eleven. My vision had come back enough that it wasn't affecting my game at all. But that first season was challenging.

We had a pretty good team, but my game had elevated to the point that even as the only freshman on a varsity team in a strong conference, I knew I could be a dominant force on the floor. However, the head coach was very loyal to his senior players who had done their time in the program. I just wanted to be on the floor to help us win, and so it was a long and frustrating high school season when I had to sit out a lot. When we played against Duncanville High School, which was one of the top-ranked teams in the state, I finished the game with sixteen points and twelve rebounds and was able to control the game. It was a big game in a season when I should have played more. I had a lot of respect for the older guys who had earned a spot in the program, but at the end of the day, I believe you put your best players on the floor to compete. There were a lot of minutes on the game clock when I found myself sitting on the bench and looking at the floor, knowing that it wasn't even close—I was the best basketball player in the gym. Even with my limited time that year, I was starting to get noticed by the national scouts and writers.

Despite the frustration, I am thankful for that season and all of its difficulties. I believe God knew the kind of leadership and mentoring I was going to need in the coming years. If my freshman year hadn't been so difficult and confusing, I might've stayed at Mansfield, but I would've missed out on some great relationships. Those challenges were preparing me to be the man God wanted me to be.

After a disappointing high school season, spring rolled around and I was excited to get back to my AAU squad. That season Team Texas was ranked nationally. Marcus Smart, Phil Forte, and the guys were coming along and colleges were already recruiting most of the players on my team. My high school season had been so brutal that I was ready to get back to playing with my friends. Playing, not sitting on the bench!

School ball had just finished up, and we were starting to practice together. We were all really excited about some of the tournaments and travel that Coach Roberts had lined up for us. I can't even describe how great it was to get out and play with my team again. The intensity of the practices was just unbelievable. Guys were really getting after it, but when we stepped off the floor, we stuck together.

I was able to compete in a few important games early in that spring season. My talent was starting to gain more national attention from the scouting services at that time. In one of my early AAU games that spring, I went against Quincy Acy, who was a junior at the time, and I scored twenty-four points. Quincy went on to play at Baylor and then to the pros with the Kings and the Knicks. He and I would later become good friends. At the time, he was a highly recruited and talented athlete, and it was one of the games when people across the country who hadn't heard of me started to pay close attention.

I had only been playing for a few weeks with my Texas teammates—it must have been during a scrimmage or at one of our practices—when something else happened to my right eye. It wasn't a particular play or a specific dunk, and I don't recall ever getting hit in the eye or anything dramatic like that. Over the next couple of weeks the vision in my right eye started to get worse than it had ever been. Again, it was like trying to see through a dense fog. It was beginning to affect my life now. It made me physically sick sometimes to think about it, as my eye got worse and worse.

Dad scheduled a checkup with the doctor, and when Dr. Kozielec examined my right eye he could no longer find the corrective lens. It had somehow dropped. He was concerned that if they didn't get the lens out, it could do even greater damage to my repaired retina. The news was devastating. Another surgery. I came home and cried—it had not even been a year since that terrible run of painful eye operations. Now I was really concerned about the future of my basketball career; I had struggled on the court with one eye, and the limited vision was starting to impact my game again.

I WENT IN for my fourth surgery in March 2009, this time to find and remove the lens. It went well, and wasn't nearly as painful as the previous surgeries. But while they were removing the lens, they discovered that my retina was peeling back again. It meant that for some unexplained reason, my eye just was not healing properly. My only hope was to undergo another surgical attempt to fix my retina. Each time we went through one of these operations, the chances of success dropped. None of us realized at the time that there might be something wrong with the connective tissue throughout my body . . . connective tissue such as my retina.

This was one of the darkest times in my life. It was the first time I started to really consider what it might mean for my dream if I could never recover my sight. I couldn't understand why God would give me a vision of playing professional basketball and then allow my eyesight to be taken away.

Another surgery? It was almost like a sick joke. My family came home from that doctor's visit devastated. Each time I endured an operation we would all get our hopes up—we kept faith that it would get fixed. I spent several days feeling down about the whole thing. Mom even started to investigate whether there were other basketball players with eyesight impairment who could give me some advice. For the first time in my life, I was faced with an obstacle that seemed impossible to get through. No amount of thankfulness, no amount of love from my family, no amount of prayer was going to fix the problem.

So this was when trust became real work. There were no answers as to why I kept facing these terrible eye surgeries. No matter how many times I prayed about it, we always seemed to return to another bad report from the doctor. If God had some kind of big plan going on in the background of my life, I definitely could not see it. My eyesight seemed like a challenge that would always be with me.

At times I felt like my eyesight was attacking my dream. No one with a vision disability like mine had ever heard their name called in the first round of the NBA draft. When I would lie down at night and visualize myself being drafted, it hurt. I could still envision myself walking across the stage on draft night, but that dream seemed a little blurred now.

I still believed, but it was taking a lot of real work to hold on to it.

I remember telling Mom that I felt like what I was going through wasn't fair. Her response was: sometimes life isn't fair. Mom said that she couldn't understand why God had put this in my path either, but that we all needed to trust Him. The kind of trust she was talking about in that moment is the tough kind. It really takes a lot of work. A lot of faith. There is nothing easy about it. Then she really got emotional and fired up like she can get when she's speaking from her heart. She told me that I had two choices with my vision impairment: I could quit basketball or I could work to overcome my limited vision. "Isaiah," she said, "you only have two choices here: you can make this your *excuse* . . . or you can make it your *story*."

It was my choice to make. I didn't really understand what I was learning about trust at the time. Perhaps God was trying to teach me the importance of trusting Him through adversity. Trust is all about holding on to a vision when the road ahead is blurry. My faith was new, and I was forced to look deep inside myself and decide whether I thought God was going to do something positive with this situation or not. I had to come to terms with the fact that just because I couldn't see the good things God was doing, it didn't mean He wasn't busy working behind the scenes. I could easily relate to this because of what I was going through physically at the time.

Each of the obstacles I had faced was a story, if I would choose to embrace it. It was a new mind-set, a way of looking at things. It came down to my choice. Was I going to let this vision impairment take away my real dream? Could my impaired vision take away my life vision? I knew what Mom was saying. I had the power to make the decision. I could work to overcome this disability, or I could let it get the best of me. I couldn't control what had happened, but I could control my reaction to it. I could make this obstacle my excuse or make these challenges part of my story. I didn't have a doubt—I was going to continue to trust in God.

And I was going to make whatever happened to me *my story*.

CHAPTER 5

WALK BY FAITH

I feel like everybody who chases a dream comes to a place where they just don't think they can make it. At this point, the odds were stacked against me. I struggled a little on the basketball floor now that my vision had gotten worse. There were two ways for me to go after my dream: I could be the first player with a known disability to walk across that stage on NBA draft night, or I could keep going back for more operations, hoping that it would work out and my vision would return. It was the beginning of my sophomore year in high school, we understood that my retina was peeling back again, and Dr. Kozielec said I needed to get the surgery done quickly. It was a tough decision.

Being blind in one eye would mean that my depth perception would be off, and it would impact every area of my life. As difficult as it was to deal with in my everyday life, I knew it would be a huge feat to conquer on the basketball court. I had been an unbelievable passer, but now I could only see half the floor. At nearly seven feet tall, I had been able to bury jump shots from all over the court, and now I was struggling sometimes not to airball a free throw. The idea of overcoming this challenge seemed impossible, but the very idea of another surgery was more than I could even bear to think about. To this day, I absolutely cannot stand to sleep on my stomach because of how much time I had to rest like that after each surgery. I also didn't know if I could deal with the pain again . . . it was so intense. Most important, I wasn't sure I could handle the emotions of having my hopes crushed by one more failed surgery.

We prayed about it as a family. We prayed about it with Pastor Goines. And then I locked on to this one verse in the Bible that I heard one Sunday morning at church. It was 2 Corinthians 5:7, "*For we live by faith, not by sight.*" I remember hearing that verse and it just stuck with me for a long time. I couldn't stop thinking about those words "not by sight." If I was going to make this disability my story, I was going to have to trust in God. My parents and I talked about the idea of trying just one more operation. Then we spoke with Dr. Kozielec, who had been so supportive throughout the whole process. Mom, Dad, and the doctors thought it might be worth another try, even though the chances of success were very slim.

Looking back on it and understanding my condition today, I am not sure another operation would've helped. Somehow I knew that I couldn't go through it again.

My life was going to be truly difficult if I were to accept the blindness in my right eye—but I was also determined that I was going to be great at basketball no matter what happened. At that point, I could still make out shapes and movements from my right side, but it was quickly getting worse. It was one of the hardest decisions I would ever make, but I was not going through another operation.

I felt somewhere inside me that it was time to just accept it. I needed to make my eyesight part of the vision for my life. I believed that God had given me my dream in the same way he had given Joseph his dreams. I sat Mom and Dad down and told them that I was done with surgery. I was going to make this my story; I was going to "walk by faith, not by sight." We told Dr. Kozielec that we would see him for a checkup in a couple of months.

Dr. Kozielec is intense. He's a fighter and he wanted to keep trying, but he was also supportive of my decision. After years of trying to save my vision, the surgeries were finally over.

I feel like God knew what I needed at that point in my life. I didn't understand why He didn't heal my eye, but I was going to overcome this. And He brought some people into my life during this time that helped show me how to handle my new disability.

DURING THE SPRING of my eye operations, my parents were busy looking for a different school for me. They wanted me to be in a place where I would be challenged on the court *and* in the classroom. Grace Prep Academy had a solid basketball program and a great coach, Ray Forsett, who had a tough, no-nonsense approach to teaching. Mom and Dad liked him immediately. Mom appreciated how focused the academics were at Grace Prep. It was a college-like atmosphere with smaller classes. We would only go to school three days a week, and the other two days we were expected to do reading, homework, and meet in our study groups. The two days off also gave me extra gym time.

I first met Uncle Dre at the Grace Prep gym that summer going into my sophomore year. He was coaching an AAU team, and everyone in Dallas seemed to know him. Dre loves to help kids. He was good friends with Coach Ray, so he was always hanging around the Grace program. Dre is an energetic guy who loves to be around people. He's always laughing and I don't think he's ever met a stranger. He and I formed a close bond quickly after we first met. Every time I saw him around the gym, we would talk about our families. Uncle Dre has this big voice, so if he was in the gym you could hear him talking and laughing. He was always easy to find—even in the loudest gym. One day he walked by and seemed upset. I asked him what was going on, and he explained that his wife had cancer. After we talked for a few minutes, I asked him if I could come by the house and visit with them.

Later that week, I met Aunt Evelyn. She was in the middle of her battle with cancer, but when I walked into their home, it was so full of joy that you couldn't tell that anyone was sick . . . and she was *really* sick. Aunt Evelyn became one of my favorite people from that day forward. She was going through chemotherapy at the time and had lost all of her hair. Some days she didn't have the energy to even get off the couch. But she was still laughing and smiling. When I started to drive my sophomore year, she was right in the middle of her fight with the disease. On days that we didn't have class, I would drive to their house to hang out with her and watch television. I wanted to keep her company while Dre had to work, especially when she felt sick from the cancer treatments.

I was also right in the middle of my own struggles. The vision in my right eye was getting worse each day. It was as if the light was just getting dimmer. The decision not to try another surgery meant that my retina would quickly become totally detached and my eye would die. By the beginning of my sophomore year that process had already begun. It wouldn't completely die until my senior year in high school, but from my sophomore year on, I was pretty much blind on my right side.

I had taken my eyesight for granted. I struggled to do simple things, like pouring myself a glass of water. At school, it was hard to walk through hallways or around desks without running into things. I even had a difficult time walking through my own house! I would run into furniture on the way from my room to the kitchen, and as a teenager, I was always going to the kitchen to get something to eat. Mom is one of those people who likes to rearrange the furniture in the house quite a bit, but she couldn't do that anymore because it made it more difficult for me to get around.

Can you imagine training yourself to do the little things that you take for granted, like pouring a drink or fixing a sandwich? When I wasn't on the court playing, that was my life now. I was even scared that I wouldn't be able to get my driver's license. It was difficult for me to shake hands with people because I wouldn't be able to see clearly where their hand was, so I had to practice those types of everyday tasks for hours so that I didn't embarrass myself in public. I had to learn new ways to survive everyday life, and it was hard work. I would get frustrated at times—if I struggled with normal tasks, how would I ever overcome the bigger challenges?

Seeing Aunt Evelyn deal with cancer was a huge help during this time. She was inspiring—she seemed to attack cancer the same way I would attack people on the court. Her faith in God was unbelievable; it was like she just trusted that God was walking with her and holding her hand through each doctor visit, each treatment, every high and low. She was confident everything was going to be okay, no matter what happened. She didn't let bad days get her down. And she had some really bad days. Aunt Evelyn and Dre quickly became close with my parents. Evelyn was my inspiration, even before she and Dre became part of our family.

One day after visiting her, I came home and asked Mom to take me to the store because I wanted to buy a nice ladies' scarf. I didn't know anything about that sort of thing, and I needed help because I wanted to get one for Aunt Evelyn. Mom looked confused. I guess she thought I was buying it for some girl at school, but I explained to her about Evelyn and how she wore scarves on her head because she had lost her hair during the cancer treatments. Mom helped me pick out a good one, and I took it over to Evelyn and Dre's to give it to her. She likes to remind me that when she opened it I said, "A beautiful scarf for a beautiful woman." I thought that my aunt Evelyn was one of the bravest people I had ever met. Even through her cancer battles, she and

Dre kept everyone smiling and laughing. Before long they were sitting with my parents at my basketball games and we were all spending Friday evenings hanging out at their home and playing games. I decided to get a cancer awareness tattoo to remind me of how much Aunt Ev means to me. I'm not sure I could've handled all of the new physical challenges without watching her example of how to deal with life when it hits you with bad stuff.

It was a battle every day to learn how to handle life with my disability, but basketball presented an even bigger challenge. I had always lived on the basketball court. I had put hours into practice. Now, blind in one eye with no depth perception, I had to work even harder.

And I did.

I went from shooting hundreds of shots to shooting thousands. I was on the court every waking second, whether it was in my driveway or at the gym, because I could no longer count on my eyesight to get the ball in the basket. No one was going to watch me play and be able to notice that I had a disability. I had to retrain my mind to remember the distance from the three-point line, the free-throw line, and around the basket. My best friends, Elliot and Elijah, helped me work through these challenges, because if you wanted to hang with me, you had to spend time on the court. While neither of them were big basketball players, they would rebound while I put up thousands of shots. Whenever I got down, they were in my ear telling me that I could do it. They would never let me forget that I could be great.

And when I was out there playing, my teammates helped me. I became more dependent on them, especially at first, to know where they were going to be on the court or to know when a screen or a double team was coming. I played with some great players at Grace Prep Academy, such as Jordan Mickey, Emmanuel Mudiay, Karvair Shepherd, Drake Thomas, and my man Je'lon Hornsbeak. I also began to understand how important it was to communicate with my teammates on the defensive end of the court. Thinking back now, this is when I really started to understand the game of basketball in a bigger way—more like a coach than just a player. You could say my "basketball IQ" began to really grow. Because of my limited sight, I could no longer only be concerned with just what I was doing, I had to have a much better grasp on what was happening at every position on the court (both offensively and defensively). For example, I had to *know* where my guys would be when I caught the ball on the block so I could set them up with the right pass, because I couldn't always count on being able to *see* them anymore. So when I say I can *see* the game better than most players, it began with my need to overcome the challenge of having limited eyesight. That process was still tough. There were a lot of moments early on when I came off the court frustrated because I couldn't do the things I had done with clear eyesight.

But I just kept at it.

The first time I went to one of Coach Ray's practices I thought he was crazy. We all did. I don't think we touched a single ball. He yelled at us and we ran the entire practice. He was on us so bad that at one point I took my glasses off and threw them on the floor and may have even told him he was crazy. He quickly got in my face and explained how I was going to learn to take care of my business on the court. I walked out of the gym after that first practice thinking to myself, "What have I gotten into?" But we had a group of good players, and Ray knew that with our schedule he needed to bring us together as a team. And he did.

Coach Ray was also real intense about our grades. When we were at school he would come by a class to see if we were paying attention. He knew if his players earned a bad grade on a quiz sometimes before we did. And if we messed around in school, he made us run. If we cheated, he made us run. If we skipped a class, there was going to be more running. Believe me, that kind of stuff didn't happen more than once, because everybody knew the consequences. Ray held us accountable on and off the court. There were no excuses in his book . . . *ever*.

But Coach Ray believed in me. He would tell me, "You made it this far, so why give up? You have a special gift. Keep pushing, keep working!" It was our relationship off the court that helped me trust everything he said to me on the court. Coach Ray was all business between the lines in the gym. But no matter what happened at practice or in a game, Coach Ray always left it on the court. Outside of practice we would talk basketball only when I wanted to talk about it. He always made it clear that he was concerned about me as a person first and as a basketball player second. Ray would sometimes drive me home after practice, and I could always talk to him about anything going on in my life: girls, church, family and friends, school, whatever. His advice and friendship as a coach and mentor had a huge impact on me as a player and a man.

I WAS STILL actively being recruited by Oklahoma State, Texas, Kentucky, and Baylor. (We didn't tell any of the coaches about my vision impairment, because even with it, I was able to dominate games; it became a "family" secret.) I was so impressed with Coach Drew and the family atmosphere at Baylor every time I visited that I didn't want to drag out my decision about college. As players for the biggest Christian university in the country, teammates at Baylor would pray together at the end of each practice and have Bible study together every week. Mom simply loved that the academics there are great.

The family atmosphere was the thing that separated the basketball program from the other schools on my list. You can't walk into a Baylor practice, even today, and not notice it. The coaches treat the players like family; the program treats the families of each player and even the former coaches of their players like part of the family. Coach Drew and Coach Mills cared about me as a person first, a basketball player second. Coach Drew sets the tone for his team with his unbelievable positivity. I believe this is why he was able to lead Baylor basketball out of some rough years.

I felt comfortable on campus and didn't see a reason to drag out my decision. It was also a big positive that I would be close enough for Mom, Dad, Noah, and Narah to come to all of my games. I wanted to focus on winning championships at Grace with Coach Ray, so I fully committed to Baylor University during my high school sophomore season. It lifted a weight off my shoulders and let me focus on what was really important.

At this point, I was working through how to play with my limited eyesight. I was seven feet tall and even with my disability could still handle the ball better than most grown men. I was still highly ranked, but that part of it started to explode as I began to get more press around the Dallas area. My sophomore season I was named one of the top three prep players in America. We visited teams in different states, playing games against the best prep schools in the country.

There was one particular game when we were playing in Tampa and I had to go up against James McAdoo, who had committed to North Carolina. It was a battle. He was older than me and a talented big guy who also played on the perimeter. Our styles were similar, and that meant we went head-to-head for big parts of the game. I really got the best of him on one particular dunk during the game. I more than held my own against him; I finished that day with a double double and we won the game.

With all the success we had that season, my sophomore year ended with a lot of disappointment. We easily played our way into the Texas state semifinals. Our guards could apply pressure because I could rotate to the goal so quickly to block shots. We rolled through the tournament with high hopes, only to lose the semifinal game on a last-second half-court shot. The team was really upset about the loss; it was a heartbreaker. I thought about it every day that following summer. I didn't want to let it happen again.

Coach Ray can be tough on his players, but he's also really good about coming back around and making sure you are okay. I knew he had my best interests at heart for Isaiah the person, not just Isaiah the basketball player. He would invite me over to dinner with his family, and he also became somebody I could talk to about anything. Ray says I am the hardest worker he's ever coached. I would always get to practice early to work on post moves and jump shots, and would stay after for as long as I could to do the same. But that spring and summer after my sophomore year, I took my work on the court to an even greater level. I would call Coach Ray in the morning and tell him to get his butt out of bed so we could do some work. It wasn't anything for him to meet me at the gym at seven in the morning and for us to put in a full day of practice.

Coach Ray also introduced me to Coach Pops, Ray's dad, who would be around practice. Sometimes Ray and I would go over to Pops's house for dinner. Coach Pops is a deacon at his church and a very spiritual man. He does a lot of work with basketball, but he also drives a truck for a living. Whenever he was on the road, he would call me to check in and see how life was going. Every couple of days he would call late in the evening to tell me he was going to pray for me. God continued to surround me with people helping to grow my path spiritually and who would be there with me through the good and bad times.

WHEN MY JUNIOR year at Grace started, I was hungry to wipe that semifinal loss in the Texas tournament from my memory. I was still ranked by a lot of people as one of the top prep players in America, but I was too focused on the season to think much about it. Coach Ray made sure our schedule was even tougher that year than it had been the year before. That year he introduced me to Mo Williams, and I was putting in hundreds of hours of extra work at the Academy. My disability didn't seem to impact my game. If you were really watching, you might see me miss a free throw from time to time or not see a rebound, but even my Baylor coaches who watched me on tape said that you had to pay close attention to even notice.

The one game that stands out to me during my junior year was when we went to play a prep school in Lubbock, Texas. It was a close game when I pulled up for a jump shot right at the buzzer. It miraculously went in and we won the game.

The biggest moment of my junior year in high school, though, was the tournament we played at the City of the Palms during winter break. We were down by twenty points to Mater Dei High School, which was the top-ranked program in the country. Coach Ray grabbed me at halftime and really got onto me. He told me it was time for me to take over. I remember him telling me that there were no excuses. My disability didn't matter. He said it was my time. We came back from twenty points and won the game. I was able to control my plays on both ends of the court and shot eighty percent from the floor. It was a victory well earned. The next night we upset another powerhouse team, Monteverde Academy. Coach Ray tells me that I played like a superhero in those two games.

We qualified for the Texas state tournament again that year and went all the way to the semifinal game. We were playing the same team that had beaten us the year before. The matchup was so physical that at one point I was given a technical foul for throwing an elbow. I felt that I was only retaliating for a nasty cheap shot from one of their players, but it seems like officials never *ever* see the first guy, and they always catch the second. We won the game, but I had been ejected and was disqualified from playing in the final, championship game. I had worked all year to get back to that game and now I had to watch it from the bench. Emmanuel Mudiay was a freshman that season and he came out and dominated the game. We won the championship that year, and I was happy for Coach Ray and my team, but having to sit out left a bad taste in my mouth. I made a choice to use it as motivation. I wanted to get back and play one more time.

As one of the best prep players in the Dallas area, I would get interviewed on television from time to time. Doing those interviews at such a young age was great experience for me. I was never really nervous about the interviews and enjoyed talking to the media. At this point, my eye had completely died. It had changed color and was starting to droop a little bit. It was especially hard to deal with because I didn't like the way it looked. Mom and Dad bought me some glasses that I always wore at school to hide my eye. I wore protective glasses when I played on the court that did the same thing. Those sport glasses started to become my trademark while I was still playing in high school. I remember sitting in the living room one night with Mom, and we were watching an interview I did with a local sports reporter after a big game. I saw myself on television and it made me pretty upset. It was obvious on TV that something was wrong with my eye, so it had to be obvious to people when I was talking with them in person. I wanted to do something to fix my appearance so that people wouldn't notice.

We called Dr. Kozielec, and he recommended that we see Dr. Randy Trawnik, a doctor who makes prosthetic eyes. He's a cool guy who lost his own eye in a military accident, and he keeps an office in Dallas and Germany. He actually hand-sculpts prosthetic eyes to fit his patients so that they look real. Dr. Trawnik designed my eye so that when I would look down at people—which, being seven feet tall, I do all the time—my eye would still look normal. I remember when I first put it on, Mom cried. It made me realize how hard she had taken all of those surgeries. The eye is removable and needs to be professionally cleaned, but for the first time in a couple of years, I didn't have to walk around hiding my bad eye and I found a new confidence. I felt more comfortable with my appearance. It wasn't that I was interested in hiding my eye from everyone; I just wanted it to look normal, like everyone else.

The day I went in to get fitted for my prosthetic eye, Dr. Trawnik had closed his office to the public. I walked to the waiting room with my parents and saw Lauren Scruggs, the model who had been terribly injured by an airplane propeller in Dallas. She was also there to get her prosthetic. I had the chance to talk to Lauren a bit while we were in the waiting room, and she was just an inspiring person. It was cool to meet her that day.

Going into my senior year at Grace Prep, I was on a mission.

My goal was to win another state championship and to be there on the floor when we cut down the nets. Coach Ray arranged our toughest schedule yet, and we went into our season ranked as one of the best high school teams in America. I was ranked by ESPN as the number-three prep player in America, right behind Nerlens Noel and Shabazz Muhammad. The team ran through the season. It was time for the state tournament again. We made it back to the semifinals, and I played some of my best basketball of the year. When we took the floor for the final game, I was completely focused. There would be no dunking before warm-ups to get me ejected—no elbow to get me thrown out of the game. That game was more like an All-Star game than a championship game. We jumped out to a big lead and just beat the brakes off them. Cutting the nets down after that state title is still one of my favorite memories.

As spring rolled around I had two unbelievable experiences: I was invited to play in the McDonald's All-American game and in the Jordan Brand Classic. The McDonald's All-American game is an All-Star event for the upcoming freshman class of next year's college basketball season. I played for the West squad and we won, 106–102. I scored ten points and pulled down eight rebounds in just seventeen minutes on the floor. The game was fun, but I will never forget spending time with the kids at the Ronald McDonald House. It was heartbreaking and inspiring to be around the children battling illness. We baked cookies with them and took them out to play ball. I walked away from that experience praying that we brought some joy to their house that day. I know being around those brave kids brought all of us a lot of joy.

Next up was the Jordan Classic. I had ten points and eight rebounds in the game, but it couldn't touch what happened before we actually came out on the floor to play. As we arrived at the arena before the game, the coaches and organizers of the Classic directed the bus drivers to take both teams to a back entrance. They told us the usual way in was "too crowded." We walked down a maze of hallways until we got to a room with nothing but a desk and a chair. We were all looking at each other wondering what was going on. Everybody was hoping that we would get to meet the man himself, "His Airness," but they had told us before we arrived that he wouldn't be available. The next thing we knew, the door opened and Michael Jordan walked in . . . the greatest player in the history of the game. I noticed he was wearing these sweet baby blue Jordans with his name on the back and that he wasn't wearing any of his championship rings. When he first walked in he looked at us real seriously for a minute and then broke out in a big smile and asked us why we were all being so quiet. He went around the room and introduced himself to each of us and shook our hands. I really don't get nervous around famous people—they are just like you and me—but this was Mike, and I was actually shaking a little from excitement. When we shook hands I just couldn't believe how big his hands were. It was a great moment.

In those couple of weeks of downtime after the All-Star games, I thought about how close I was to qualifying for the NBA draft. I was just one year away and not far from my dream. I thought about all that I had been able to overcome. My senior year I had gotten a tattoo of the Bible verse 2 Corinthians 5:7 that had inspired me to embrace my blindness and make it my story. . . . My dreams were close, but that meant it was time to work even harder. I was headed to Baylor as the most highly rated player ever to commit to the university. NBA rules stated that I only had to do one year of college before I could be eligible to walk across that stage on draft night. The dream that began when I was a kid in California had grown so real that I could almost feel it.

I left Grace Prep excited about my new adventure, but thankful for the three years I spent on the campus with Coach Ray. Grace Prep had brought me so many great memories; it was also the place where my family and I had grown up. I couldn't imagine my life without my friends from Grace, without Coach Ray, Coach Pops, Dre and Evelyn. In a lot of ways, Dallas now felt the same as Fresno had when I was young. It is tough to leave a place like that, but as Dad had told me years ago, sometimes you have to leave a good place to find success. My dream was close and I was walking by faith.

CHAPTER 6
ONE AND DONE

I had overcome a lot to get to play NCAA basketball, and through the encouragement of my family, I was able to stay thankful and focused, but something happened my freshman year at Baylor. For the first time in my life, I lost myself. The pressure of what I was trying to do on the court got in the way of me remembering who I was and the values my family taught me. All the lessons I had learned from my parents, Coach Ray, Aunt Evelyn, Uncle

Dre, and my friends drowned under the pressure I felt to succeed. I arrived on campus with high expectations on my shoulders. I had been embraced by another great family-like situation at Baylor. I had been on campus so many times during my junior high years that it didn't feel like a brand-new place to me. I already knew all of the coaches and their families pretty well, and they were all acquainted with my family. Coach Drew makes the program such a family atmosphere that I think everyone's moms, dads, brothers, and sisters feel comfortable being around campus and visiting with the team. I was also familiar with the guys I would be playing with before I even stepped foot on campus. My best friend from high school, L. J. Rose, was coming to campus to play ball, too. The situation at Baylor just felt like my home away from home.

The problem was that I went to Baylor not really focused on the incredible opportunity I had to represent a great school and to play for coaches I had respected for a long time. I got caught up in the noise about being a lottery pick in the NBA draft. I allowed the criticism of my game from the media get to me. I treated Baylor more like a place that I was renting for a year, just a stepping-stone on the way to my dream, instead of as a part of my family that was trying to help me to achieve my dream. I had a "one and done" attitude going into my freshman season.

Even when I arrived on campus that first summer, my recruitment had gotten so much attention that I was already well-known. People would stop me and ask for my autograph as I walked around campus. Seven-foot-tall guys like me can't sneak around. I spent that summer working hard, as I had always done. As soon as I got to campus, Taurean Prince, one of my new teammates, and I hit it off right away. L.J., Taurean, and I were all roommates, so the three of us always hung out together. We were going to have a great team that season, but my dream of the NBA was so close that I was always focused on how my own individual performances were going to affect my position in the upcoming draft.

I might've been the guy with the hype, but it was clearly the squad of the point guard, Pierre Jackson, at the beginning of the year. It was an adjustment to come into a team that had a lot of pieces already in place. I hadn't ever been in a situation where I had to find my role on a team. This was the first season in my life where I wasn't going to be the go-to guy on the floor. Practice was physical and competitive. Cory Jefferson, Rico Gathers, and I made up an unbelievable front line, but I wanted to be out on the floor at all times. I couldn't stand to sit on the bench, which got to me right away when we started playing that season. I'm such a competitor; I wanted all forty minutes on the floor. When I didn't get the time I wanted, I would get upset. Coach Drew sat me down in his office and explained that they had a rotation cycle and there were certain times when I would have to come out of the game. He said it was best for the team and that he was never going to compromise what was best for the team. I didn't buy it. I wanted to win, but I also wanted to showcase what I could do on the floor. I don't mean to say that I was selfish all the time, but I was a perfectionist and hard on myself. When things weren't going well on the floor, it affected my attitude. I also believed we had the best chance of winning when I was out there on the court.

The Baylor coaches had always known about my disability, but they didn't truly understand it until I arrived on campus, and I never felt like it affected my play. I started off the season playing pretty strong. I remember in one of our first games against Lehigh University I came out with ten points and twelve rebounds, a double double, in just a couple of minutes on the floor. We played Boston College the next game, and I had sixteen points and nine boards. But then I struggled with an ankle injury. For me, having to sit on the bench was hell.

Baylor started out the season okay, especially with an early win against Kentucky at Rupp Arena on December 1, 2012, but then we went on a losing slide. We were piling up losses and it was frustrating. Coach Tang, one of the assistant coaches, was coaching me hard and getting on me at practice and, honestly, I didn't take it well. I would get upset at myself for missing shots or not making good plays, and then the coaches would get after me, and it just felt like it was too much to handle. When a coach would correct me, I wasn't hearing what he was teaching me in that moment. I would also be hearing the criticism I was getting about my game from the so-called basketball experts in the media. Sometimes I would respond in a really bad way. It was the first time in my life that I fell into talking back to the coaches, and I am definitely not proud about the way I behaved during some of the games and practices. It seemed like I still had a lot of growing up to do.

If you got in trouble at practice, the coaches would send you to the strength coach to cool off and do push-ups as a punishment. We were still losing that winter and weren't working together as a team. We dropped games to College of Charleston and even Northwestern. I was so frustrated that I just lost my temper one practice. I lost my cool in such a way that I hadn't before. The coaches sent me off the floor and Coach Charlie and I really got into it. Coach Charlie is Baylor's strength coach. We call him "the Punisher," like the character from the Marvel comic book, and we even have T-shirts for him with the comic book's skull symbol on the front. He talked me down after our altercation and we hugged it out and moved on pretty quick.

The whole time that things were going bad with the team, I was also putting a ton of pressure on myself, because I desperately wanted to be a top-five lottery pick. My head wasn't thinking about the good of the Baylor team; I was distracted and focused on myself. I fell into a bad place during this time of not trusting God, not trusting my teammates, and not hearing my coaches. I felt like all of a sudden my dream was so close, but it was all up to me. Mom would say I quit trusting. I would get really angry sometimes on the floor, so much so that I wouldn't be able to calm myself down.

Here I was surrounded by a group of coaches who cared about me as a person. But with all the pressure I was feeling, I just couldn't focus on all that I had to be thankful for in that situation. Coach Drew is one of the most amazing people I've ever met. I mean, we are talking about a guy who took over a program where players were killing each other with tension and turned it into a real family. A lot of other programs talk all that stuff about being a family, but if you visit a practice it is obvious—those coaches at Baylor believe it. It's part of who they are as people. Even today, I don't understand why Coach Drew doesn't get more respect. He's taken the Baylor program to two Elite 8s and a Sweet 16 and won the NIT championship, but he still doesn't get nearly enough love from the national media. I was on a Christian campus where people treated me like I was one of their own. Coach Tang, Coach Nuness, Coach Mills, and Coach Maloney are solid guys that have my back. I was also surrounded by some of the best teammates I had ever played with, but all I could focus on was getting to the NBA.

There were a couple of moments that year that allowed me to step back and understand where I was going wrong and helped me to start turning things around. We were getting ready to play

Kansas State in the Big XII play but still struggling as a team. At practice the day before the game, I had one of my weekly battles with Coach Tang. Coach Tang isn't shy about dealing out the truth on the court when he needs to, and he's not quiet about it either. I was so frustrated that I tweeted something like "biggest mistake ever" without really thinking about it afterward. In that moment, I was just so emotional that I wasn't thinking clearly. I felt like I should've never come to Baylor. At this point in my career, I had come to college with all of this hype, and things weren't working out the way I wanted. I was getting some grief from the media for my play on the court and battling through an ankle injury; I wasn't impacting the game like I knew I could. This built up on my shoulders and weighed on my mind day after day. I definitely wasn't clearheaded when we arrived at the Kansas State arena. The team was shooting around and practicing when Coach Mills came over to talk to me.

I met Coach Mills when I was in the seventh grade and liked him right away; we've always been close. One time, he tried to sneak in and watch my eighth-grade practice. My coach had invited him, but told him he needed to sit really high up in the stands so he wouldn't be noticed. Right in the middle of my practice I saw him and yelled "Coach Mills?" and had to go give him a hug. My eighth-grade coach wasn't happy with the interruption of practice, but I've always loved Coach Mills. Even when Coach Drew had just taken over at Baylor and the team was struggling,

Dad would drive me down for games and Coach Mills would invite me to the offices to say hi to everybody. He says he remembers me as a tall, lanky, goofy-looking junior high kid walking through his offices after a game wearing my Carmelo Anthony jersey.

Coach Mills cut straight to the point during practice that day at Kansas State and called me out on sending the tweet. He asked me what I was doing. I didn't have a good response. He told me that my outlook was wrong and I needed to fix it. He told me that Baylor was everything I needed and I was ignoring the positives: I was around a family, I was close to my home, and I was playing for coaches who cared about me and wanted the best for me. He said, "Isaiah, Baylor is your home, too, and you need to stop treating it like rented space." Coach Mills is another one of those guys I consider family, because he's always going to tell me the truth. I felt terrible. I apologized and deleted the tweet as fast as I could.

Our conversation didn't really change the fact that I was letting the pressure get to me. The "draft experts" believed that I was falling out of the top five lottery projections for the NBA draft, and it was hard for me to listen to that kind of negative talk. Combined with the fact that I was faced with losing on the court for the first time in my life, the whole situation was rough. When I was making shots and things were going well, I was okay, but when I messed up and Coach would bring me off the floor, my emotions would take over and I could have some bad outbursts. That's when Coach Mills sat me down after practice for another talk. Like I've said, there is nothing more important to me than being a role model for little kids. He told me that his kids were noticing my behavior when I came off the floor. You see, the thing I didn't think about when I was so emotional was how my outbursts were affecting the people who sat behind the bench. My temper and body language were so bad sometimes that Coach was telling me his kids had noticed. It was a big reality check for me. I was embarrassed about my attitude and behavior. I didn't want to make excuses for the way I was acting, but I needed to grow up and I knew it. I promised Coach Mills that I would fix it right away and I did.

The rest of the year didn't seem to get better for me or our team, but I worked to do a better job of hiding my frustrations. We had a ton of talent, but no matter how hard the coaches worked, for some reason we couldn't pull it together. There were some fun personal moments in the season, like the time we went into Rupp Arena, in Lexington, Kentucky, and walked out with a 64–55 win. Kentucky had recruited me a bit when I was in high school, and there was something cool about going in and beating them on their historic home court. We were a really good team that night. I had eleven points and, defensively, we just owned them. We held them to thirty percent shooting for the game. The hardest part was that the game occurred early in the season and gave us a taste of what we could achieve before we started losing. It made our losing streak even tougher to know that we had gone into Rupp and won that game.

I also enjoyed getting to play against some of my high school friends on the college level for the first time. When you grow up playing with the same guys your entire life, it is pretty special to look across the floor and see them representing a big-time program. Je'lon Hornbeak and I are close friends, so whenever we would play Oklahoma there was a lot of funny talk going back and forth between us. When we played against the Cowboys I'd get to see my guys Phil Forte and Marcus Smart. Phil is an unbelievable shooter and Marcus is a beast out on the court. During one of the first games I played against Marcus he tried to dunk on me. I didn't let that work out too well for him. Marcus and I have always been pretty tight, and honestly we don't really clown or talk that much smack to each other. Whenever we face off in games, both our families are there, so we usually say things on the free-throw line like, "How's your mom?" or "How's your sister?"—that kind of thing. Usually after a game, our families get together and hang out.

Baylor finished a tough run through the Big XII with a win over Kansas in the final regular-season game. Going into the Big XII tournament that year, the experts said we were on the bubble for an NCAA tourney birth. Baylor had to win two games in the conference tournament to guarantee our place in the big dance.

After the year we had, we all felt there was a chance to turn the whole season around in just a weekend of games. I was still projected in the first round, but was feeling some pressure to play my way back into the top of the lottery. We went out in the first game against Oklahoma State and just played terrible. Let me rephrase that: I played terrible. I picked up two fouls early and ended up finishing the game with only two points. I was upset with myself after the game because we lost by only one basket, and I felt responsible for the loss.

We were still hopeful that we had enough quality wins to make the field, so when Baylor was left out of the selection on Sunday the team was understandably upset. It's hard to get news that you aren't invited to the big stage when you've worked so hard for it as a team. It is your goal all year. It was devastating to be left out. There were some good things happening around the team at that time, though. Getting snubbed by the selection committee brought us together as teammates. And we were invited to play in the National Invitation Tournament. And we were determined to win it.

A long time ago, before there was an NCAA tournament, the NIT was a big deal. It used to be the tournament that determined the national championship. It has a lot of history behind it, and the final games are always played in New York City at Madison Square Garden. In college basketball today, the NIT doesn't have anything to do with determining the best team in the country. It is a postseason tournament for the teams that didn't make it into the NCAA tournament field. Mom would've said that we decided to make getting snubbed by the NCAA selection committee "part of our story." We wanted to get to Madison Square Garden and show everyone they were wrong for leaving us out of the top sixty-four teams. We didn't live up to what we had wanted to do that season, but the truth was that our strength of schedule and our talent were still good. As a team, we felt disrespected and angry. We showed up to the gym that week and were all business. Everybody was together and focused on one goal. As a team, we had a huge chip on our shoulders.

We played angry that entire tournament; we truly played our best ball. Something else happened, though. I stopped worrying about the draft and focused on my team. Pierre was our senior leader, and he set the tone early on in the NIT. Cory, Rico, and I dominated the paint. We took our frustration out on Long Beach State in the first round, beating them 112–66 at home. We rolled through the NIT, beating Arizona State, Providence, and BYU to advance to the final game, against Iowa.

It was an overwhelming experience to play at the Garden. Coach Maloney is from New York, so he was like a little kid out there. The Garden means so much to everybody who plays ball, but especially to guys from New York City. To them, the Garden is like some kind of basketball holy place. We easily beat

Iowa in the championship game. Pierre played one of his best games of the season with seventeen points, Cory Jefferson had twenty-three points, and I finished with fifteen points. I left it all on the court that game. The coaches told me later that they felt like I had played my most complete floor game of the year, rebounding, blocking shots, and shooting well. We won the game by twenty points.

It was an incredibly special night, getting to cut the nets down at MSG. There are only two teams in college basketball that end their basketball season with a win, and that year the Baylor Bears was one of those squads. As that last game ended, so did the pressure I'd felt all season. I had put in my time for my team and learned something about myself. The dream I had fought for my whole life was just months away from becoming a reality. And we came together as a team and played up to our potential.

A week or so after the tournament, I was out in Los Angeles with Coach Ray for a basketball event, and I talked with Coach Drew to tell him that I was leaving for the NBA. Coach Drew was supportive and said he was behind me one hundred percent. As disappointing as my freshman season was, my agent, Dwon Clifton, felt that I still had a good shot to be drafted in the lottery. I finished up my school responsibilities and moved back to Dallas to stay with Aunt Evelyn and Uncle Dre so that I could work out with Ray, Jay, and Sweat at Mo's Academy to prepare myself for the upcoming NBA workouts.

I had worked all of my life to get in this position, and I wasn't going to give up now. I had a couple of weeks to get even better before the NBA workouts. I was feeling confident. I headed over to Mo's gym on a weekday to go through my routine. Coach Ray had some guys watching me work out that day just to see some of the training routines they would put me through at the Academy. It was standard routines like footwork, shooting drills, and post moves. I was doing some post moves and Sweat passed me the ball. I squared to the basket and was ripping the ball through while Jay hit me with the pad, and I would go up and finish the play. He wasn't hitting me hard, just giving a little bit of resistance while I caught and turned into my move. On my first demonstration catch as I turned into the blocking pad, I heard something pop in my shoulder. Nothing really hurt at all, but I immediately dropped the ball. Jay threw it back out and when I tried to catch it I just couldn't. Something was wrong with my shoulder; I couldn't use it anymore. I stood there in disbelief. I hoped that the pop I heard wasn't anything serious.

We rushed to the emergency room to get it checked out and Dad met us over there. My parents were in the process of packing up to move to Kansas at the time. As I was being wheeled in for the X-ray, I was arguing with Dad about buying myself a new car. He and Mom had helped me buy a new car with the money we saved for my college education before I came to campus freshman year. I was telling him that I wanted to get something new since I was going to be a lottery pick, and he was getting frustrated because in his mind there was no need for new wheels. That's my dad—always being practical. I was excited because some of my buddies who were already in the league had some pretty nice rides. We were arguing about it when the doctors took me in to diagnose my shoulder. I told him that I'd buy what I wanted to buy after the draft. These proved to be some famous last words between Dad and me.

As you know, I don't have a lot of good luck when it comes to doctor's visits. I started to get a bad feeling as they examined my shoulder. The doctor told me that I had torn my labrum. It sounded like something I could manage, but then he explained that it would mean surgery followed by a six-month recovery, and I wouldn't be able to work out for any NBA teams. I couldn't believe my ears; after everything that I had already overcome . . . another obstacle? I sat back wondering why this kept happening to me. Ray and I called my agent, and he began talking to the different NBA teams about where I might fall in the draft if I couldn't work out because of my injury. The consensus was that I would probably be a late first-round pick. That wasn't my dream. I had put all this work into my dream, and I wanted to be a lottery pick.

We wrestled with the decision for a couple of weeks. Mom's company had transferred the family to Kansas City and so my parents drove down to Texas so that we could all meet the day before the deadline for me to declare for the draft. We called Coach Drew to tell him that I wasn't sure that I was going to declare. We were supposed to fax our paperwork to the NBA by midnight that evening. I spent the whole night weighing the pros and cons and was still up in the air on my decision until late in the evening. I finally decided at 11:57 p.m. that I was not going to place my name in that year's NBA draft. Coach Ray kept telling me that it didn't matter where I went in the draft, it mattered what I did after I was drafted. For some reason, I didn't want to hear his encouragement. I wanted to go in the lottery. It had a lot to do with all of the pressure and criticism I had faced my freshman year at college. I wanted to go in the top five so I could prove all the critics wrong. I watched the clock hit midnight and knew that my dream of being drafted was now another year away. I made the decision that it was best to go back to Baylor for my sophomore year, but it turned out that wasn't such a sure thing either.

When I told Coach Drew that I had decided I wasn't going to enter my name in the draft and was hoping to come back to Baylor for another season, he said that we needed to have a meeting. The guys on staff had decided that they wanted me back, but with some conditions. If I was coming back for my sophomore year, I had to make some changes. Even the thought that Baylor might not want me back was tough for me to deal with, I had always been the go-to guy—I was always the one that everyone wanted on their squad.

We scheduled a meeting at Coach Ray's house to discuss the conditions of my possible return to Baylor. The Baylor staff came down to meet with me, and we sat around and talked for a while about what the expectations would be when I returned to campus. It was a hard meeting for me. Whenever you have to face up to things you have done wrong, it's tough. I knew I had made some mistakes with the way I handled myself my freshman year. The coaches explained to me that they needed the Isaiah who played in the NIT, not the one with a bad attitude who was eaten up by pressure during the regular season. I knew in my heart that they were right. A lot of my behavior freshman year just wasn't a good look for me. I was better than that. Coach Drew and those guys were there because they cared about me, but honestly, it was hard to hear.

I left the meeting still feeling pretty angry. I wasn't mad at the coaches as much as I was disappointed with myself. I talked with Coach Ray, and he told me in the most honest way that only he can: I was going to have to change. When I talked to Mom about the whole scenario, it hit me even harder. She said I had gotten myself into a mess and was going to have to man up and get myself out of it. Everyone at the meeting said how they felt and held nothing back. In the weeks that followed, I went from being angry and disappointed to understanding more about myself. I started to see how wrongly I had approached that season. I had let all the noise around me drown out what was really important. My Baylor guys had the courage to do what family does, and that's telling each other the truth. As I came back to campus that summer, I realized that I didn't like who I had let myself become in the past year. I sat down and talked with Coach Tang, and he helped me understand the specific areas that I needed to work on. I had become so focused on being a top-five pick that I had forgotten what really mattered. The next time I stepped foot in Baylor's gym, I would be coming home to family.

My freshman college year wasn't what I imagined it would be, but I wouldn't trade that season for anything—especially our NIT title win. It was the year I finally grew up. I realized how easily you could lose your life vision when you start to focus your sight on the wrong things. I gained a new maturity and learned valuable lessons I hope to share with younger players to help mentor them. I learned that an important part of trusting God is to focus on doing the work that He puts right in front of me to do. My dream was still alive, but I would just have to be patient and be the man that Mom and Ben had raised me to be. I didn't think it was going to be easy; I just needed to revise the vision of my dream.

I was returning to a strong Baylor team with a dominant front line my sophomore year. We had ended the season in New York City on a mission, but there was plenty of unfinished business . . . family business. I was going to be sidelined for months rehabbing my shoulder, but I wanted to work to make my teammates better. I was coming back to Baylor focused on my team. I wanted to make this the most memorable season I ever played.

CHAPTER 7

"41"

I began my sophomore season at Baylor with high expectations for myself. The pressures and criticism hadn't changed, but my focus was completely different. I had grown up quite a bit. I wasn't just coming back to Baylor basketball, I was coming back to my Baylor family. I didn't know what was ahead of me, but this would prove to be one of the most important years of my basketball career and a big turning point of my life. Mom's advice about knowing the difference between believing in God and trusting Him stayed with me, and the year ahead would teach me more about what it meant to trust God.

The summer was difficult because I was sidelined the whole time rehabbing my shoulder. I couldn't play and I couldn't work out like I was used to. It was frustrating, but it also let me step back from the game and learn some lessons that I couldn't have learned while I was out there competing on the court. Ever since I was a kid, when I take the floor, a switch goes on and my competitiveness completely takes over. It's the only way I knew how to play. It's also one of the things that has always given me an edge and made me a great player. I learned early in the year while I was sidelined that it was also something I needed to learn how to control. I needed to have some perspective.

I would still show up to the gym every day to rehab with the training staff. It was hard work, because the recovery process was slow. My team was working out and playing, but I couldn't participate. I started coming to the gym to help the coaches. I would officiate the games and get water for the guys while they worked out. I began to learn more about myself during that time I stood off to the side. For the first time, I was showing up to the court, not to compete but to watch and support my teammates. I've always been a student of the game, but I was usually in the middle of the action. While I sat out, I started to view the game a little differently. I began to think about it from the standpoint of not just what I could do better as an individual player but what I could do to help make my teammates better.

Since I couldn't work on my game, I started calling up my guys Taurean and Rico and rebounding for them while they worked out. I watched how Coach Drew, the leader of our program, would be the guy to hand out waters and towels to the players during a break in practice. Our coaches are servant leaders, and because I was on the sidelines with them during those months, I started to understand what that meant. I've always been serious about watching film. If I see a guy make a move I like in a game I will get the tape and go back and watch it until I get that move down. Now I started to watch film to help my teammates get better, too. It reminded me of my first eye surgery. You don't understand how much you love something until it is taken away from you. Those months while I was injured, my love for the game grew more mature. If anything, having to sit out grew my obsession with basketball.

My rehab wouldn't be over until right before the season started, so it was going to be tough to be ready to go from day one. You can run sprints all you want on the basketball court, but it is a different level of energy when you are out there competing. You are also running on the court with four other guys; there are all kinds of parts to the game that you get used to depending on who you are out there with. That's something you can only pick up while out there scrimmaging. I was going to have to work hard to get myself back to game speed. Since it was a shoulder injury, I knew that my shot was going to be affected, especially early on. We had lost Pierre Jackson to the NBA, but I felt like we were bringing back some good players. I had changed my perspective on getting to the league. I still had my hopes set on draft day, but I wasn't going to go into the year feeling the pressure to prove I was a lottery pick. I think a lot of young players in my position should learn to block out all that pressure and focus on one practice at a time and one game at a time. The NBA will find you if you are taking care of your business and focusing on the right things. I wanted our team to pick up where we had left off in the NIT the season before—to jump out of the gate and just clown people.

We started out strong that season. Kenny Chery was running point and our front line was solid. We went to Maui to play in a preseason tournament in November and beat several good squads to get to the championship game against Syracuse. I played one of my best games in Maui against Dayton, which turned out to be one of the better teams we played against all year. Cory, Rico, and I were tough to deal with out there on the court. Baylor had a long, athletic, and physical team. We finally lost our first game of the season, to Syracuse, but the trip to Hawaii was awesome. To spend time on the beach there and go sightseeing were great ways to spend Thanksgiving. It was a paradise out there.

RIGHT: I was involved in sports from an early age—playing baseball when I was ten years old.

LEFT: Being over seven feet tall had its advantages on the court.

RIGHT: My trademark became my glasses when I played at Baylor. Here I am—game-day intense in a game at Kentucky.

LEFT: Winning the 2013 NIT championship with Baylor was also a dream come true.

RIGHT: Smiling with my sister and brother—Narah and Noah.

BELOW: Slamming a dunk in a game against Nebraska.

SECOND AND THIRD ROU

LEFT: With NBA commissioner Adam Silver on the infamous NBA draft night at the Barclays Center, Brooklyn, New York.

RIGHT: The moment my dream came true—when Adam Silver announced my name as the NBA's honorary draft pick of 2014.

LEFT: Talking with the press on NBA draft night on June 26, 2014.

LEFT: Posing with the cast of *Good Morning America* in June of 2014.

RIGHT: After conducting a raw and emotional interview for the *Today* show with Robin Roberts and Mom (Lisa Green) the morning after the draft.

LEFT: With the cast of *SportsNation*— Marcellus Wiley, Michelle Beadle, and Max Kellerman.

LEFT: The people that mean the most to me: Dad (Benjamin Green), Mom (Lisa Green), Narah (sister), and Noah (brother). We were attending my first annual "Evening with Isaiah Austin" fund-raiser on October 24, 2014, to support my nonprofit organization.

RIGHT: Owen Gray (second from right) and his friends, also diagnosed with Marfan syndrome, at the fund-raiser to help raise money for the disease.

BELOW: Auction items up for bidding during my first annual "Evening with Isaiah Austin" fund-raiser to help support the Isaiah Austin Foundation.

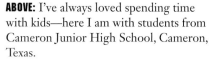

ABOVE: I've always loved spending time with kids—here I am with students from Cameron Junior High School, Cameron, Texas.

LEFT: Signed basketballs to be included in the auction for the Isaiah Austin Foundation.

BELOW: A family photo—from left to right—Carly, me, Narah, Noah, Jenna, Grandma Shirley, Ben, Anna, Matt, Lil Mac, Lindsey, Andy, Melissa—2014 in Wisconsin Rapids, Wisconsin.

LEFT: Meeting President Barack Obama in July 2014 was a huge honor.

LEFT: The NBA made a jersey for me featuring my number, 21.

ABOVE: Signed basketball from NBA commissioner Adam Silver.

LEFT: I was invited to attend the 2014 ESPY Awards in Los Angeles.

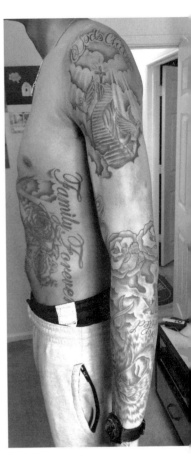

RIGHT: One of the ways I honor my faith in God and my love for my family is through my tattoos. I have several meaningful Bible verses and references to family tattooed on my body to remind me of what's important.

LEFT: Family Christmas photo in 2014—Me, Lisa, Narah, Noah, Ben, and the family dog, Elise.

Baylor was climbing the rankings and getting noticed when we hosted Kentucky on December 6 at AT&T Stadium in Arlington, Texas. The game was hyped up since we had beaten them the year before, but like most teams each year, this was a completely different squad. Kenny played a great floor game that night and led us in scoring with eighteen points. The crowd was decked out in Baylor green that night. They were crazy loud and into it from the beginning of the game; I don't know if we were feeding off the energy our fans brought that night or if they were feeding off the energy we were bringing to the court, but we jumped up on the Wildcats 16–7 in a hurry. Kentucky was a talented team, though, and we knew it would be a battle. It went back and forth until right before the last television time-out; Kenny went to the free-throw line and hit a couple of shots. Then I slammed a dunk to put us ahead for good. Cory and I finished with thirteen points apiece, and ESPN reran my dunk on *Sports Center* all week. We went back to Waco feeling like we had a legit shot to win a national title. The Kentucky win left us confident that we had what it took to beat anyone in the nation.

We came back from Christmas break ranked in the AP poll as the seventh-best team in the country. As a team, we were excited to get into Big XII play and prove how good we were. The Big XII that year was going to be a tough grind. In my opinion, it was the best conference in the country that season, top to bottom.

Every team had guys who were going to be high first-round draft picks. The great thing about the ten teams in the Big XXII was that you got a chance to play every team at home and away. It was a balanced schedule.

We dropped our first one to a strong Iowa State squad and then ran over the Texas Christian team from up the road in Dallas. But that's when things started to get tough, like it had been my freshman season. I was still facing a lot of criticism from the basketball media. Everyone was saying that I made the right decision to come back to college. It seemed as if all the experts on television wanted to take a minute to criticize my game. One analyst, a former Kentucky assistant on ESPN, even called me "soft." I was still struggling with the aftereffects of my torn labrum and had a hitch in my shot. It's difficult to ignore that kind of criticism, but rather than getting upset about it, I let it drive me even harder. Our whole team—coaches, players, and everybody—took it personally.

There was something different about the chemistry of that sophomore-year squad, and we were really close. We were learning to trust each other on and off the court. Coach Drew and the coaches do some cool team-building exercises at practice. One of the things they encourage us to do is to share stories about our biggest challenges in life and be up front and honest with our teammates about our struggles. One of these exercises involves having the whole team do "wall sits" while holding on to a medicine ball for three minutes. It's a tough exercise. During those three minutes, a member of the team stands off to the side and shares the biggest life challenge he has had to deal with. When the time is up, Coach Drew will ask us questions about the talk to make sure we were really listening. He wants us to get to know each other. These exercises helped cement an unbreakable bond between us as a team.

At that point in the season I was getting tired of all the criticism from the national media. I had never been open about my disability and being blind in my right eye. My Grace Prep family and some of the Baylor guys were the only ones who knew the whole story. My friend and teammate Gary Franklin encouraged me to be open with the entire team about it. Most of the guys knew, but I had never taken the time to explain the challenges I had faced before coming to Baylor. I always believed what Coach Maloney would tell me: "You only get five seconds to feel sorry for yourself every day. Only five then it is time to go to work." I never wanted anyone to feel sorry for me on the court. I just wanted to play my game.

After one practice, Coach Drew gave me the chance to open up to the guys about my experience with the eye surgeries and to share a painful part of my life; he thought that sharing my story would help bring me closer to the team. The fact that I was willing to be real honest about my struggles encouraged the other guys to talk about their lives, and it built a lot of trust with our squad. After this, I decided that I was ready to share my story with the national media.

On January 17, 2014, ESPN ran a special about my life story and the fact that I was blind in my right eye. The way people responded to it changed my life in a lot of ways. First, and most important, I started to realize how many lives I could impact by being a role model. I began to get thousands of e-mails and letters from parents and kids who had similar disabilities. I had spent a lot of time not wanting to share my story, but I had never dreamed that it could help others. Before each game, I would now have the chance to talk with kids who were facing all kinds of challenges. One of my favorite dudes was a guy named Carter. I first got to know him through my good high school friends Sarah Beth, Kate, and Emily, who used to take me to church with them on Wednesday nights. I had met Carter's dad, C.J., who was the youth pastor at the church. Carter had had an accident when he was five or six years old and lost his right eye. He came down for a few Baylor games, and he and I got to talk a little bit about it. He told me that people would stare at his eye, and I told him that was normal. It happened to me, too. When Carter was wearing an eye patch, I came out for warm-ups wearing one, too, so he would know I was thinking of him. I took the floor for a lot of games that season inspired by Carter's toughness.

I had always been focused on never letting anything, even my limited eyesight, get in the way of my vision of my future, but I never saw my story as inspiring. I was just working to pursue my dream—working for something I loved. I didn't feel like I was doing anything different from what a lot of other people would do. The response to the ESPN special was unexpected, but it also put me in the limelight as a spokesperson and a role model. I realized what a positive influence I could have on other people. The greatest part was that people were reaching out to me to tell their own stories, which lifted me up and inspired me.

Sharing the story about my eyesight also took a big weight off my shoulders. After my story came out, it seemed like the opinions of my performance on the court changed. I took pride in not allowing my disability to affect my game, and I don't think my play changed at all, but the opinions about what I was doing on the court sure did. I received some sincere apologies from analysts that I liked, such as Jay Bilas and Fran Fraschilla, who had been critical of my performance in the past. More than anything, my story helped remind a lot of the national media types that I was a person they didn't know all that well and not just a basketball player. It seems like after the story ran on national television, I just felt freer on the court. Getting it out there took the pressure off and helped me to focus on what was important. Now I am grateful for the chance to be a mentor and role model to kids who are dealing with their own disabilities. Only through sharing my difficulties was I able to help others.

As cool as the ESPN experience was, the rest of the season

wasn't going well for us. In January, things got even tougher for our team. We hit a bad six-game losing streak that started in mid-January, and it just didn't seem like we could break out of it. Baylor dropped in the rankings, and it felt like no matter what we did, it just wouldn't work out for us on the court. But this experience was a lot different from the slide we had the year before. I noticed the guys were taking it hard. *Everyone*, even the guys who didn't get much playing time, was in the gym early and staying late, trying to fix the losing streak. We dropped games to Oklahoma, Kansas, Texas, and then a heartbreaker to West Virginia at the end of the month.

One of the cool things about playing at Baylor is that we do devotions together as a team. We have a team chaplain, Pastor Brewer, who handles a lot of them. Pastor Wible, a pastor at a local church who I'm close with, also gives some of these talks when we are at home. When we are on the road, Coach McCasland (we call him "Coach Mac") or Coach Tang usually trade off the responsibility of leading our devotions. We were on the road when Coach McCasland began to tell us a story about his best friend and how his family had been devastated by cancer. It was one of those real-life emotional talks that hits way deeper than just basketball. It hit me hard, because I knew from watching Aunt Ev how terrible cancer could be. Then Coach Mac started talking about Chapter 41 and one of my favorite Bible characters, Joseph. We read through the story about God using

Joseph and his dreams to save Egypt from the famine. We talked about how Joseph rose out of all the different kinds of trials to be the Pharaoh's right-hand guy. Coach shared what his best friend was going through, and we all locked on to the story. The guys all started to talk about Chapter 41 and how important it was to take care of business and keep our focus on our dreams even when things around us were going bad. It fit in with what was going on with a lot of us personally off the court and also the losing streak we were on as a team. Chapter 41 became more than just a devotion that we did on the road—it became our motto. Even as we were dropping in the national rankings and the Big XII standings, we stayed committed, just like Joseph did when the chips were down. We focused on trusting each other and trusting God. Everybody was putting in the work. There was no finger-pointing. We were focused on the message in Chapter 41. It meant a lot to me because of my experience pursuing my dream. In my two years at Baylor, this devotion would be the one that seemed to change everyone on the team the most.

We started February with a big win against Oklahoma State. It felt like maybe things were starting to turn around. Our goal all year was to qualify for the NCAA tournament. We were hungry to get back to the way we played at the beginning of the season in our game against Kentucky. We played Kansas on February 4, and they just rolled over us. We prepared for that game feeling confident, so it was a frustrating loss. I wish you could've been in that locker room. When everybody is working so hard to get wins and you keep losing, guys can start to bail out on the team. There was none of that. We just kept looking to each other, knowing that we could turn it around. People on the outside were starting to talk about the NCAA tournament, and if we continued the way we were playing, there was a good chance we would not make the field. But we just kept on believing in one another. That's when we traveled to Kansas State.

We went into that K-State game knowing it was a must-win. Bramlage Coliseum, the "Octagon of Doom," in Manhattan, Kansas, is a tough place to play. We got there early to shoot around, and I joked with Coach Mills. The last time we had been on this floor, I was a different person. The game was an absolute battle from the tip-off. We ended up playing into two overtimes. Baylor was down by three with time running out. There were just seconds left when we ran a play and missed the three-point shot that would've knotted up the game. Cory grabbed the rebound and put up another shot, but he was way inside the three-point line. We had to sink a three-point shot. I knew when it left his hand that it was going to miss to my left side of the basket, so I started banging my way in to get position. I knew what was on the line, and there was no way I was going to let anyone in a white jersey pull it down. As I went up to get the ball, I knew that my man Brady was spotted up and waiting to shoot just beyond the arc. Brady Heslip was 0–8 at that point in the game. Some guys would think twice about not passing it out to him, but that didn't even cross my mind. I knew the clock was running out and I had the best shooter in the country open at the three-point line.

I grabbed the rebound and kicked it out to Brady, and he did his thing. He had been putting in the work every day; I would trust Brady to make the shot a thousand times over. He let go of it real quick and I knew when it left his hands it was going in. He just straight up cashed it. That shot saved our season. We've talked about that game a lot of times since. All the coaches say that was the one play that helped turn our season around. We jumped on K-State in the second overtime and won the game. Kenny had twenty points and played great. Taurean had twelve off the bench, Cory had twenty-one, and I finished the game with eighteen. That particular game broke us out of our streak. After that we got back to playing like the team that beat Kentucky in December.

When the Big XII tournament started we felt like we were solidly off the bubble, but the first-round loss the year before when I fouled out with only two points had left a bad taste in my mouth, and none of us wanted to leave any unfinished business. I had struggled offensively all year because of my shoulder, but by the time March rolled around my shot was coming back. We didn't get a first-round bye, which meant that we had to play the first day and it would take four games to accomplish our goal. We wanted to win the conference tourney and build momentum for the NCAA tournament. We didn't have any problem taking care of business against that Dallas team in our league. On Thursday and Friday we beat Oklahoma and Texas. I was shooting the ball in rhythm and playing the best I had all season. By the time the championship game came around against Iowa State on Saturday night, we were completely out of gas. It was our fourth game in four days, and the other team came and shot the lights out. It felt like they didn't miss a three-point shot all game. Iowa State was a great team that year. The loss was disappointing, but it wasn't disheartening. As a squad, we all felt like we had done Chapter 41–type work. We had kept at it; we had trusted each other and survived adversity. We were ready for the big dance.

Our draw in the first round of the tournament had us playing in San Antonio, and when we took the floor for our game against Nebraska, half the arena was wearing Baylor green and gold. The NCAA tournament is a special experience—they put you up in nice hotels, you get a tour of the city, nice dinners, and it is all first class. Nebraska was a tough, grind-it-out kind of squad, and we had some nerves early on, but we still won our game without a lot of stress. In round two, we ran into Creighton and the Naismith Player of the Year candidate, Doug McDermott. From the tip-off we overmatched them. We were too long and athletic for them, and Coach Drew had a great game plan. We took away the corner shooters with our length and conceded the free-throw line, but they couldn't get shots over us in the paint or even make a jump shot from midrange all night long. The game was like the perfect storm. We were smothering them defensively, and offensively we were hitting on all cylinders. They just couldn't guard us at all. We had all five starters in double figures in that game. I was 7–11 from the field and finished with seventeen points. We beat the brakes off that team.

Cutting down the nets to advance to the Sweet 16 was an incredible feeling. If you watch our celebration after that game, the thing you can't understand unless you were part of our locker room was that it had everything to do with Chapter 41. We had kept the faith when things were bad and were celebrating our win as a family. I was so happy for the coaches. They had put so much work into getting us to that point. Coach Drew, in the post-game interview with Craig Sager, asked if everyone could rub his hair for good luck. It was a good moment and showed a little bit of Coach's laid-back personality and sense of humor. Coach Drew gave his players all the credit during his postgame interviews for the press. The coolest quality about Coach Drew and the Baylor guys is that when they talk like that, they aren't doing it for the cameras. They are the hardest-working coaches I've ever been around. They are also the most unselfish group of guys you will ever meet, and when things go right, even when the reporters aren't around, they make sure to give us the credit.

We went into that Sweet 16 feeling confident that we were

ready to play. We felt like the Wisconsin Badgers were one of the best teams we had faced all season. They had the length to match up with us and could spread the floor and shoot the ball. Still, we felt like we were the faster squad if we could rebound and get ahead of them. Wisconsin came out hitting shots and moving the ball so well that our zone, even with its height, didn't seem to bother them. We played one of those games on offense when we couldn't find the basket. Some of it was that they were a good defense team, and some of it was us not shooting the ball well. Sometimes that happens when you are playing, and you hope that you can force the other team to struggle from the field, too.

It all went wrong that night against Wisconsin. They played the perfect game to beat us, and we didn't do ourselves any favors. I hate to lose, but they deserved that game. We walked away from the loss feeling like we had been knocked out of the tournament by a solid team. Wisconsin ended up advancing to the Final Four that season and losing on a last-second shot to Kentucky. It was still a hard loss for us, though, because we knew Kentucky was still out there and we knew that we could beat them. It was also difficult because none of us wanted our time together to end—especially with a loss.

I can count on one hand the number of times I've had to finish a season on a loss. I've been lucky to play on some great teams. The locker room after the Wisconsin game was tough, but not because we lost and were done for the season. We had bled together that season. We had been through the worst and over-came it together. Basketball is funny like that sometimes. You can have a great season and never develop that kind of brotherhood in the locker room. The end of our tournament run was emo-tional because we knew that was the last time we were all going to line up together. It was the last time Kenny, Cory, Gary, Royce, Brady, Taurean, and I were going to be on that floor in green. We came home to a crowd of fans at Baylor, and while I'll never get over losing that one, I eventually started to appreciate what we were able to do that year as a team. It was special.

We were on the way back to Waco when, for the first time that year, I began to turn my attention back to the draft. I had truly "lived" at Baylor that year. It was no longer a school I was passing through on the way to the NBA; it was my home, and these guys were my family. I had overcome so much in my life, but I felt like I finally grew up my sophomore year. Chapter 41 would be something that I would lean on in good times and in bad for the rest of my life. Baylor basketball was always going to be a part of me.

When I arrived back on campus, I knew it was time to take care of business. I sat down with Coach Drew, Coach Tang, Coach Maloney, Coach Mac, Coach Nuness, and Coach Sam to thank them for what they had done for me. I told them it was time for me to go. Cory and I would both be entering the draft process in the months ahead. We had become close that season and were going to push each other to get ready for the NBA. Next year's Baylor Bears squad would be a different group and would rely on Taurean, Kenny, Royce, and Rico. It was going to be their squad and their chance to add to the Chapter 41 history. I took care of business with my classes and made my way back to Aunt Evelyn's in Dallas to begin preparing for the NBA draft. The road to accomplishing my dream had taken a lot of turns. I had overcome a lot of challenges that no other player had ever faced. Now it was just a matter of time before I would hear my name called on draft night . . . I was going to be the first player ever drafted in the first round with a known disability. I was standing right there at the edge of my dream.

CHAPTER 8

AT THE EDGE OF THE DREAM

It was finally my time. The dream that I had held on to and fought for since I was a kid in Fresno was so close. I was staying in Dallas to get ready for the NBA combine. A lifetime of unexpected challenges had taught me to take nothing for granted. The adversity I had fought through had helped me understand that though I was standing at the edge of my dreams coming true, it only meant it was time to work harder than I ever had before.

131

In that month leading up to the draft, I was putting in ten-hour days. I worked out at the Academy with Ray, Jay, and Sweat. I would put in a full day of strength training, skills training, and then most nights would try to get back later and put up thousands of jump shots. I couldn't stand the thought of one bad shooting performance at a tryout. I was obsessed with preparation. No one was going to outwork me, and I was going to show up for my auditions in better condition than anyone else. At the outset of that spring there was a lot of talk that I could be drafted in the first round. But I knew it was all talk.

A lot of work goes into preparing for the draft. I knew I was going to attend the NBA combine on May 14, and I didn't want to waste a minute. Putting in six days of work every week was nothing new to me. Sometimes people believe when you are seven feet tall that God has gifted you enough that all you must do is show up. It's true, my height has given me an advantage, but without my work ethic, I would never be the player I am today. A lot of my success came because I naturally love the game more than most people do. Since I was a little kid, practicing basketball has been an everyday way of life for me. I never thought there was anything unique about it. It was always an escape for me. I never would pay attention to time going by while I was on the court, unless it was during Coach Ray's crazy sprints. All that to say I've never felt like working hard at my dream was anything special. When you love something, that's just what you do; you work at it. My work ethic grew intense starting in high school because I was exposed to elite athletes from the league. Mo, Ray, and the guys in Dallas who invested in me showed me the level of commitment it takes to make it. Since then, I've always wanted to outwork everyone I know in the gym. I've always believed it is important to bring it to every drill.

That spring, as my name was being mentioned as a possible first-round pick, I was also getting more press because of my disability. I don't even really like to say the word "disability." To me disability sounded like a weakness, and my vision had really become my source of strength. It is what drove me to work harder than anyone else. I would dare people to feel sorry for me on the court while I was out there embarrassing them. But the ESPN story in January, which had shared my story about being blind in one eye, had made quite an impression. I continued to give interviews about how I had overcome it, and it gave me the chance to reflect on what I had accomplished on the court since my eighth-grade year, when I began dealing with limited eyesight.

People always seem to be amazed and want to talk about the fact that my blindness *doesn't* impact my performance on the court. Most of the time, people who deal with vision problems have their entire lives to learn how to make up for them. Doctors have talked to me about how a lot of their patients who are sight impaired have had years to learn to compensate with their other senses. They grow up learning to deal with the depth perception challenges and other obstacles from their limited sight. I had never given it much thought. I had turned my adversity into a positive. I never had the greatest vision to begin with and I wore glasses almost my whole life. When I completely lost sight in my eye, I was determined that it wasn't going to get in the way of my dream. There had been an adjustment period, but I was able to overcome it with my work ethic. I don't understand all the mechanics of it. I've always put in hours and hours of repetition. My sight didn't change the mechanics of my shooting at all. I just had to learn the "feel" of each distance, the right force to use from each spot on the court, because I couldn't completely rely on my eyesight.

I take a lot of pride in the fact that I can shoot the ball better than most guards who are playing with both eyes. The only time my limited vision seemed to impact me was when I played in big arenas with a lot of distance behind the backboard. Some of the NCAA tournament venues can be like that, but I never felt like it hurt my shooting from the floor in any of those games. I just had to show up extra early and get more shots up than usual so I could get my vision adjusted to the background. Playing in Allen Fieldhouse at Kansas bothered me sometimes because the goal was so close to the crowd and there was so much going on behind the basket in the way of colors and movement during the games. My foul problems there bothered me more than any shooting background. In my mind, I'd never given a lot of thought to the fact that I could play with one eye. I wasn't anything special. I did what anyone else would who loves what they do: show up every day and get after it. I wasn't going to let my struggles get in the way of my dream.

The only fear or concern I've ever had about my vision since I became totally blind in my right eye was the possibility of losing the other one. The thought of that happening has always scared me to death. I wear protective glasses when I play, and I've always felt fortunate that I never took a hit to my left eye. I didn't ever anticipate that being a problem on the court, though. I guess it was a trust thing. I always figured that God had had me experience enough adversity in my life. He wasn't going to let me be completely blind. I believed that I had earned some protection from anything else ever getting in the way of my dream. And as far as the things I could control personally, I was going to be ready.

I had met my agent, Dwon Clifton, years ago when he was coaching at Baylor. He became close with my family and has always been in my corner. He was excited about the prospects of my draft position even before the combine. Dwon, Ray, and everyone else in my camp were convinced that once I got out on the floor for the workouts, I was going to play my way into a solid first-round selection. I was working in the gym to put weight on. Coach Charlie had worked hard to get my weight up during college, but I was a little light for a player of my height. I still had a lot of advantages, though. I was really long and could do things with the ball that other big athletes competing for the draft couldn't do. I believed that no other big guy could shoot, pass, or handle the ball quite like I could. I wasn't just a "five" who could stretch the floor. I could take you to the block and do some work, too. My postgame had come along in my time at Baylor and I had turned into a good shot blocker. I led the Big XII in blocked shots during the conference tournament in my last run.

Dwon was communicating with teams, and we submitted my paperwork for early entry into the draft without hesitation. I was in Dallas most of the time, but I would go down to Waco to visit my girlfriend and hang out with Taurean, Cory, and some of the guys. When I was in Waco, I would play ball with the team and Coach Tang had some awesome pro-level workouts he would put Cory and me through as we would spend time in the gym after hours. Baylor was still my home, and whenever I visited I tried to spend some time catching up with Coach Drew and the guys.

I put in thousands of hours of work in that spring and flew to Chicago for the NBA combine on May 14, 2014, ready to make a great impression. Players don't *have* to attend the combine. It is a voluntary thing, and your performance there usually isn't going to make or break your draft status. My guys felt like it was a good decision for me to go, since it would line me up against players who were projected higher on the board than I was, and we were all confident I could outplay them. I went hoping to make some noise and prove myself.

The first days of the combine focus on a bunch of drills. It isn't much different from a lot of the basketball camps I had gone to in my life. The scouts and coaches divided us by position and did a lot of the usual drills like running weaves, different cone drills, a lot of shooting, and fast-break drills. Some people think the combine is like open gym and they divide you up and let you run pickup games. That would've been so much fun with the talented group of players there, but they never do anything like that. When you do actually play, it is focused on three-on-three situations and you are going against similar position guys. The coaches who run the combine keep you moving from test to test, and there isn't a lot of downtime once you arrive. I was performing well and having a lot of fun.

The combine is also the place where doctors poke you and conduct all kinds of tests to determine your fitness level. They make you do a vertical jump with and then without a step; they make you bench press, measure your height, weight, wingspan, and body fat. I measured at seven feet and 220 pounds, which was nowhere near what I needed to be.

That year, some of the testing was a little different. It was the first year that the NBA was going to run certain heart and blood testing as a part of the combine. I went through the medical evaluations and didn't think much about them. I didn't even think about my long history with doctors.

The combine was a fun experience, because I also got to do a lot of interviews and meet new people. I enjoyed that part of it, but I loved being able to prove myself as a skilled player with true talent the most. When you're playing as a post player, even on the perimeter, you can show off your shooting skills over the course of the season, but it isn't a naturally consistent shot in any college offense. Scouts never got a great look at the damage I could do from a distance by watching tape from my Baylor seasons. I thought that I would be able to create a buzz at the combine with my shooting touch from distance and my ball skills. For the most part, that's how it worked out. I was sure I was going to come out of the combine with a lot of teams interested in inviting me to individual predraft workouts. Unfortunately, the medical tests messed up that whole plan.

I got back to Dallas and was so excited. It was May 17, and the draft was just a month away. The top-ten picks looked solid. It is hard to play your way into that high of a position, but I was focused on creating buzz with my individual workouts. My plane had barely touched down in Dallas when I received a call from Dwon. He said that he had just gotten off the phone with the general counsel for the NBA and that I would need to return to Chicago to undergo further testing to determine whether or not I had Marfan syndrome. The arteries in my heart were enlarged and I had been flagged. This also meant that I dropped from a possible first-round pick to being a ghost. I would completely vanish from everyone's draft board. I sat there on the phone for a minute with Dwon not able to believe what he was telling me. This was not God's plan. It couldn't be right.

I had heard the word "Marfan" years ago as a junior high kid in Minnesota, but I also remembered that I had undergone plenty of testing and was cleared to continue playing basketball. My first thought as we were talking was to get back to Chicago and get those tests done as soon as I possibly could. Dwon was way ahead of me and had already started making the arrangements. The bad news was that the NBA was not going to let me participate in any individual workouts until after I had been examined by a specialist. This was unbelievable. There had been too many moments in my life like this one. It left me shaking my head. How could this possibly happen to me? If I couldn't participate in individual workouts, it was going to be nearly impossible to achieve my dream. I had been so faithful. I had trusted God, but at every turn it seemed I got news like this.

I took a plane several days later and arrived back in Chicago to meet with a specialist named Robert Bonow, who was at Northwestern. I talked with him about the possibilities and explained that I had no family history of this disease. He took some blood and told me about the screening process. We also went through some physical testing to make sure I could compete at workouts. As I sat in his office, the whole experience felt surreal. Whatever had come up in the test at the combine was wrong. It had to be wrong. I had been cleared to play and already tested negative for this disease when I was a young kid.

I sat in the doctor's office thinking about trust. My body was decorated with tattoos that reminded me of my faith—the Lord's Prayer was all about trusting God for everything. Verses like Isaiah 40:31, "*but those who hope in the Lord will renew their strength. They will soar on wings like eagles*" and 1 John 4:8, "*Whoever does not love does not know God.*" I had trusted God through so many difficult circumstances. This one was just going to be another bump in the road. I settled it in my mind right there. I honestly didn't worry for another minute about the test not coming back okay. I had played competitively my entire life, and I couldn't let anything distract me from my workouts. It was going to be one more quick mention in the reports of how I made my way to the NBA. It was going to be part of my story. I wouldn't let it take my focus off my dream.

THROUGHOUT THIS ENTIRE crisis, Dwon was working behind the scenes to get me cleared to work out. This was our biggest obstacle. They brought in my medical records to show that I had been cleared of Marfan syndrome when I was younger and made the case that I had played competitively all of my life with no issues. The NBA was good to me about the process. I signed some forms for the league, and then Dr. Bonow agreed, I should be allowed to continue on my path of working out until the testing brought back more conclusive results. The NBA cleared me to move forward with workouts. I was so grateful. Once I left Chicago to fly back to Dallas again knowing that I had been cleared, I never thought of the testing again. My concern was nonexistent. God had not allowed me to come this far to end my dream. I was confident that I had played all my life with none of the real physical issues that were related to Marfan syndrome, and it would all be okay. I was ready to get back to the gym and prepare.

My first workout was with the Phoenix Suns on May 29. I went to Phoenix excited about what I could prove. I was hungry to earn my place with the other big athletes in my draft class. The draft was on June 26, less than a month away, and the next few weeks would be an all-out sprint of flying to and from franchises across the NBA. I trained myself for the grind, though. It was part of what I had to do to get on that stage and have my dream come true. When teams work you out in individual evaluations, it is very similar to the combine. It is not usually just you. Most of the time they bring a group of guys in together. They test your stability and durability, they interview you to find out what kind of person you are, and they put you in specific playing situations so they can evaluate your skills. There are never five-on-five open-gym scenarios; it is three-on-three situational kinds of play.

My next workout took place with Dallas. I had already experienced some special moments traveling the country for individual evaluations, but this was one of the best. When Mark Cuban, the owner of the Dallas Mavericks and one of the investors on the television show *Shark Tank*, has local guys work out for him, he handles it like he would any other player. Rather than ask me to drive over to the workout like he could've done, Cuban put me up in the Ritz Carlton in downtown Dallas. Then he drove to the hotel and picked me up personally in his DeLorean. Man, I really like cars, so it was quite an experience to ride around town with him and talk. I learned a lot from listening to him. I worked out pretty well for Dallas, but like Dwon explained to me, I probably wasn't the best fit for the team's roster that year.

The next fifteen days flew by so quickly that it is hard for me to remember how I performed at each individual team visit. I wasn't getting any buzz with national media, but I was gaining momentum with the people who counted, the NBA front offices. Dwon was getting positive reports from my workouts. He felt like I was moving back into solid first-round territory. Earlier in the spring, there had been some conversations in my camp about staying home to watch the draft, especially if I was going to go in the second round. But I never saw it happening that way. My vision had always put me on the stage.

Dwon was enthusiastic about a couple of specific teams. San Antonio and the Clippers were teams he felt would be great for me. He wanted me in a place with an established veteran lineup and a coach who didn't have to worry about his job security. He said those factors would allow the franchise to take their time and invest in my development. We also both liked the Boston team—it had a great coach and was a young team. It seemed like it was a possibility, too. I kept getting rave reviews from the GMs about the things I could do with the ball at my height.

Despite going through a rough couple of years and learning how to grow up and handle the pressures of the limelight, I never doubted myself or my talent. There was a reason I was one of the top three players in America for most of my high school career. I felt like my auditions were finally showcasing my ability. But as Ray kept reminding me when we were in the gym every day, it didn't matter what team decided to pick me up, and it made absolutely no difference in what round I was selected. All that mattered was what I did *after* I arrived and unpacked my bags to go to work in the NBA. I'm still convinced that I would've been the best selection for any team in that draft. There were no other big men who could match my skill level and no one was going to outwork me. I don't mean that to sound arrogant or anything; there were some great players coming out that year, but I wouldn't have achieved my goals if I went around thinking that other guys could *ever* outwork or outplay me.

I traveled to San Antonio, Memphis, Boston, Detroit, Los Angeles, and Toronto before coming back to Dallas on June 20.

My dream was so close that I felt I could touch it. I was just a step away from achieving everything I had worked, sacrificed, and trusted for . . . I was at the very edge of my dream becoming a reality.

So this is where the story takes another difficult turn. I've already explained to you how things work with the Marfan syndrome testing. You already know that I will end up on the floor at Aunt Evelyn's house. The test would come back positive and end my playing career. Now you know what I was doing to get to this place. But in order to understand the big picture of what God was doing on June 21, the night my dream was crushed, I first have to explain what was happening behind the scenes that led me up the sidewalk with Coach Ray's hand on my shoulder and into Aunt Evelyn's house to receive the worst news of my life.

I was on top of the world when we received reports back from the Clippers organization about my workout. I was on a flight straight from LA to Toronto and then back home to Dallas that Friday. On Friday morning, Dwon had been texting me some of the great news about Los Angeles. They were interested in taking me with their late first-round selection. They thought I would be a good fit on their roster. I had told my parents and we celebrated over the phone. We were all feeling positive. I was going to be a first-round pick in the draft!

Then it happened. A few hours after receiving such great reviews from LA, Dwon received another call. It was Dr. Bonow. To this day, Dwon still gets choked up when he talks about taking this phone call. My whole crew was on a mountaintop at that point. So the phone call leveled us all. Dr. Bonow explained to Dwon that the testing had come back conclusive. He said that I had tested positive for Marfan syndrome. He also explained that if I continued to play competitively, my life could be in real danger. One shot to my chest or one extreme overexertion of my heart could kill me.

Basketball wasn't worth the risk.

Dr. Bonow called my mom to inform her as well. She received the news on her drive home from work that Friday night in Kansas City. She cried so hard that she had to pull the car over several times just to gather herself. When she walked into the house, Dad took one look at her and knew what had happened. They had to get in the car to drive to Dallas to break the news to me. Mom says that it was the longest drive of her life. She, Noah, and Narah cried the entire trip. Dad was able to keep it together until he got everyone safely to Aunt Ev's house.

There was a major operation set in motion by Mom and Dwon at this point. Everyone was working to figure out the best way to tell me. They knew how tough the moment was going to be. Meanwhile, it was Friday evening, and I was in Waco feeling great about my life. I was just five days away from my dream and honestly had never felt better. Mom, Dad, Noah, and Narah were already halfway to Dallas. My family was working to keep the story under wraps until they could share it with me face-to-face, the way it needed to be shared—with my whole family present to support me.

Mom and Dwon began to communicate with everyone who needed to know what was happening. I had driven to Waco to work at Coach Drew's basketball camp that afternoon and played in the camp game that night with Cory and some other guys. By the time Coach Drew got the call from Mom, I was already out on the court competing in a scrimmage for the campers. I had no idea it was going to be the last time I would step onto a basketball court to play with those guys. I didn't know it was the last game I would ever play in front of a packed gym. These were things I loved, things I took for granted.

Coach Drew texted Coach Nuness, who was down on the court with all of us. The Baylor staff guys were all very concerned that something could happen to me while I was out there competing. They texted back and forth about whether or not they should find a way to pull me from the game and get me off the court. At one point, Coach Nuness even tried to sub me out! I laughed him off, because there was no way I was sitting down. All my boys were out there playing and having a great time. It wasn't intense; we were trying to show off for the kids. I was playing carefree and having fun. We were doing different dunks, throwing lobs, shooting threes, and basically doing what we could to entertain the kids that night. Finally, Coach Drew called my mom and told her that I was playing on the court and he was worried about my safety. He asked Mom what she wanted him to do. She and Dwon both had the same response. They wanted me to be able to play in front of those kids one last time. I could've never dreamed it would be my last "competitive" game, but I am thankful that it was on my home floor at Baylor.

At this point, Mom and Dwon were on the phone trying to make arrangements for the meeting. They called Evelyn and Dre, because I would be staying in Waco that Friday night, but would come back to be with them on Saturday, because I still thought I was flying to Chicago for a workout on Sunday. Aunt Evelyn, Dre, Erica, and Kristina were all really upset. I call Ron and Kristina my cousins, but they might as well be my brother and sister. (My only issue with Ron is that he went to Kansas and drives around with a Jayhawk on his car; we like to tease each other all the time. He says the only time he isn't pulling for Baylor is when they play his Jayhawks.)

They took the news pretty hard, but Aunt Ev had to get prepared to host a houseful of people. Mom talked to Coach Drew and asked if he wanted to be there when they shared the news with me. A lot of coaches would've wanted to be there, I guess, but Baylor is a special place. Coach didn't hesitate, but he told Mom it wasn't just going to be him, that the whole staff at Baylor wanted to be there to support me. Coach McCasland, Coach

Nuness, Coach Maloney, Coach Mills, Coach Brewer, Coach Tang, and even Pastor Wible. The Baylor family was doing what family does—showing up even when things get tough.

Cory and I were preparing for more NBA tryouts that week and weren't all that tired from our camp game. We had asked Coach Tang earlier in the week if he wanted to work us out later that Friday evening after the camp was over. Coach Tang can put you through a crazy workout. He'd agreed that he could do it before we went into the camp game that afternoon, but when we were done with the game, he told us something had come up, and we should probably go home and get some rest. Coach Tang would never cancel something like that, so I should've suspected something was up.

I didn't, though, and we decided to head back to my apartment and hang out.

AT THIS POINT my mom was on the phone with Coach Ray, trying to figure out how to manage me the next day. Coach Ray has never lied to me about anything in my life. He still gets emotional when he talks about how hard it was for us to spend that Saturday together. He told Mom that he couldn't lie to me about anything. It was going to be difficult for him to go through the kind of day we had planned and not tell me that something was up, but he understood it needed to be done. My family needed to buy time for everyone to get to Aunt Evelyn's. After talking with Mom, Ray called up Jay, Sweat, and Mo to fill them in on the situation. Mo Williams thought it would be best to have me over to grill out at his house and keep me busy playing video games, eating, and playing with his kids. So the guys I trust more than anything in the world were the ones who scheduled my Saturday to keep me locked safe. They wanted to make sure I was busy until later that night.

There were some near disasters in all of this. Several news sources called Coach Drew that next Saturday morning while I was working out at the Academy. Someone from my camp or the NBA had leaked the news that I had Marfan syndrome and that my career would be over. Coach Drew was on the phone with a couple of the local media guys in the Dallas area and had to beg them not to run with the story. He had to tell them that I didn't know yet and that my family was worried about how I would handle the news; they didn't want me finding out while I was driving around town by myself in the car or something like that.

Mom called Holly Rowe, who had been instrumental in doing the ESPN special about my eyesight. She and Holly agreed that they didn't want my story rolling across the ticker on ESPN and disappearing the next morning. They wanted to do an interview. ESPN was interested because of the special they had run on my eyesight earlier in the year that had been well received by viewers. Our family has a strong relationship with Holly Rowe. She's a really good person and an honest journalist. She and Mom have known each other for years, and she had even babysat me a couple of times when I was a small kid. When Mom called Holly, they cried on the phone together. Mom says that she and Dad had this feeling that it was important for me to go on television and talk about it. She felt like arranging for me to take that first step right away might help move me faster toward recovering from the devastating news. I am thankful that she knew me well enough to do that. Holly grabbed an ESPN film crew and made arrangements to travel to Dallas to film my story.

For my parents, this diagnosis was much bigger than whether or not I would ever play basketball again. This was a life-threatening illness. In the hours leading up to my arrival, they were doing what most parents would. They were reading and researching all of what this diagnosis could mean for me. After the time they had to research the disease, I am pretty sure that basketball was the last thing on their minds, but they knew it would be the first thing on mine.

Friday evening I came back to my apartment after the scrimmage at the Farrell Center. I was feeling great about the Clippers news. I texted back and forth with Ray, making plans to meet him up at the gym in Dallas in the morning. That night I laughed a lot. I am not sure there was a time in my life when I had ever felt more sure about my dream coming true. I felt on top of the world. I had the chance to entertain some kids at camp, which always put me in a good mood. I had some great texts from Dwon. I was looking forward to working out with my guys in Dallas tomorrow and seeing Aunt Evelyn and Uncle Dre that night. I had one last workout coming up on Sunday, but man, the draft was just five days away now. Five days from my dream coming true. I stayed up late with my friends Royce, Taurean, and Elliot, playing video games and messing around. I went to sleep that night seeing myself walk across that stage. I even thought I knew which hat I was going to put on that night.

In reality, my lifelong dream was dead; I just didn't know it yet. Every person in my life that I considered to be part of my family was praying for me that night. Coach Mills, Pastor Wible, the Baylor coaches, Mom and Dad, Coach Pops. I know it was hard on them to anticipate what was going to happen the next night. No one knew how I would take the news. Basketball was my life. I know that there was plenty of time spent prayerfully thinking about how everything needed to happen.

Saturday, June 21, would be the worst day of my life. I had already been faced with so many challenges—from blindness to injury—but I had been able to overcome them all. I was standing at the edge of my dream, completely unaware that in a few short hours my whole world—everything I had dreamed about—would come crashing down.

Fortunately for me, my family was already there to pick me up.

CHAPTER 9

THE NEXT PLAY

There I was on the floor at Aunt Evelyn's house. My mind was racing a hundred miles an hour, wondering what could be next. I felt like I couldn't get to my feet. My head was spinning as if a three-hundred-pound dude had just set a screen on me and blown me up on the court. I had been rocked by real life, and no one had given me any warning that it was coming. I had always taken pride in my vision. I made sure my blindness was an asset that would drive me, and never something anyone could ever take advantage of, but this was a different kind of blindness. For a minute I thought of the NBA testing and wondered how I didn't see this news coming. I had been guilty of trusting . . . of trying to stay positive. "My excuse or my story?" It seemed at that moment that if there was one consistent part of *my* story, it was this kind of devastating news.

I had made it through so many trials in my life, but I wasn't sure this was something I could handle on my own. I had always been able to overcome. I had always been equipped to outwork the challenges that had come my way. Now, I couldn't even get to my feet on my own. But Ben was there, like he had always been. I thought of Fresno; I thought of God bringing him into my life. I thought of my mom with her prayers and wisdom. I still couldn't look up, but I could hear her softly crying in the background. I could feel the people in the room moving toward me. I still wanted to escape. I wanted to run out of the house and begin the whole night again. I wanted to hit the reset button on my Xbox and start the game over.

This moment in my life should've been a celebration. Instead it felt like a funeral. In a lot of ways, it *was* a funeral. My dream was there on the floor, fighting for its last breath. In a matter of minutes, my life had changed for the worse. I felt Dad grabbing me by my shoulders and lifting me up. The room was still spinning. There was crying and praying, but I am not sure I could hear anything through the grief buzzing in my head. Dad slowly put his arms around my shoulders as my feet steadied underneath me. Mom stood by to hold me from the other side to make sure I could stand. I remember Dad saying, "C'mon, son." And with those quiet words I took my first steps with the help of my parents to get up from that crushing news. I stood on the hardwood floor for a moment and steadied myself against the white walls of the entryway.

Mom and Dad helped me walk slowly down the foyer, and as I looked around the room, for the first time I clearly saw all of my family gathered there. All of the people who had helped me build this dream were in this moment with me. As I turned the corner to the left to head to the bathroom, I noticed each person in the crowd. Aunt Evelyn, Uncle Dre, my brother and sister, my cousins Kristina and Ron, Mrs. Forsett, my girlfriend Erika, Coach Pops, Coach Ray, Pastor Goines, our team chaplain Pastor Brewer, Coach McCasland, Coach Drew, Coach Nuness, Coach Mills, Coach Tang, Coach Maloney, Dwon. Everyone was wiping away tears from their eyes and looking at me to see how I would react. I needed a moment to pull myself together. I didn't have to tell Mom and Dad—they knew I needed to regain my composure before I did or said anything. They helped me turn the corner and go into the small bathroom down the hallway from the living room. The walk toward that door seemed like the longest, slowest, and heaviest steps I had ever taken. I felt like I was onstage in that moment, but not in the way that I dreamed. Dad got me into the guest bathroom and closed the door as Mom stood outside praying. There was a lot of praying that night.

When the door closed, Dad grabbed me and hugged me. That was the moment when the shock began to go away a little bit. I didn't have any words. All that was left were tears. My dream had died out there. It died in the form of some blood test in Chicago. It was gone with a report on a piece of paper and a phone call. I don't remember saying much in those moments alone with my dad. He prayed and we cried together. I began to think about all of the things God had done in my life in moments when I felt like I couldn't go on. I thought about Mom praying over me late into the night after each of those eye surgeries. I thought about the hope that grew with each surgery and the discouragement I felt every time we received the news that I would need another one. I thought about all that Ray had taught me about being a man and not making excuses. I thought about my drive to make seeing the court better than anyone, even with one eye. I thought about my Baylor coaches and how they had given me the gift of learning to trust. I thought about Chapter 41. I thought about Aunt Evelyn and her battle with cancer. I thought about Coach Pops and his late-night phone calls that could get me through so many difficult times. I thought about those brave kids like Carter. I thought about Pastor Goines, his prayers and sermons, and how he had strengthened my will to pursue my dream through the toughest times.

When Dad stopped praying, we looked at each other and I knew it was time. It was my dream, but everybody out there in that room had made a big investment in it. It was their dream for me, too. I had to go back out there. My family was waiting. The family that had been my foundation through all these trials needed to know that I was going to be okay. I didn't know what was next, but I knew the people in that room would help me. I leaned over the sink and washed my face. I looked in the mirror for a moment and thought about my eyes. I had never wanted anyone to feel sorry for me. And then I thought again about the words of wisdom Mom had given me. The words I had told everyone on the ESPN special in January. As hard as it was to realize, it was still true. I had two choices: I could make this my excuse or I could make it my story. I didn't even know what my story would look like from this point on. My story had always been about basketball. As Dad took my arm and asked me if I was ready, I remembered that my story was also about family.

Whatever was next, the people in Aunt Evelyn's living room, my family, would be the ones I knew I could lean on to help me figure it all out. I straightened myself as much as I could and I looked at Dad for a moment. *Family*, I thought. That was my next concern. Especially Noah and Narah. They were out there and they were the first people I wanted to turn my attention to. They both needed to know that no matter what happened, their big brother was going to be all right. I am not sure how, but I was finally able to gather my breath. I knew what I needed to do. Dad opened the door and Mom was there waiting. I hugged her as she cried for a moment. I needed everyone in that room to know I was going to make it through this somehow.

I walked down the hallway and stood for a second looking around. Everyone was standing and had gathered closer to the foyer. In Aunt Evelyn's house, the stairs to the second floor face the entire living room. I slowly walked around the corner and grabbed the banister, looking for Noah and Narah. They were standing right next to the stairs. My legs still felt weak, my head was still spinning, but I was no longer crying. I reached down and sat on the stairs so that I could be eye level with my brother and sister. Noah and Narah came and sat on either side of me; both of them were pretty upset. I put my arms around them and told them, "It is going to be okay. I am going to be okay." I hugged them both for a minute.

The entire group had gathered close enough that I could look at everyone in the eye. When I looked at the faces of every family member, friend, and coach, I felt I was in a huddle during a time-out of a very intense, crucial game. All I could think about from that moment forward was that it was time for the next play. Everything I thought about in my life revolved around basketball. Basketball was my identity. And my thoughts in that minute went back to the saying I would hear from all my coaches. Good players had a "next play" mentality. I had no idea what the "next play" could be. But I knew that I wanted the ball in my hands as soon as the clock began again.

I've had only a handful of times in my life outside of church services and chapels when I really felt God's presence enter a room. Sitting on the stairs at Aunt Evelyn's, I knew He was there and that I was not alone as long as these twenty-some people who were family to me remained by my side. But there was something else, something that's hard to explain. Even if everyone in that room were to abandon me, I knew God was enough for me to get through whatever I faced beyond that moment. I knew that there was a presence in that room so much bigger than all of us.

God's presence that day was not only felt by me, though. Everyone else could feel it as well. As I sat there with Noah and Narah under each arm, and my girlfriend Erika just below me, Mom touched my right shoulder as she continued to pray, Coach Pops began to sing. It was soft and quiet at first, but as everyone around the room recognized the song, they all began to join in. Coach Pops is not a pastor, but he fills that description for a lot of people who know him. He has a spiritual presence about him that shines through in the darkest moments. He had been there for me through a lot of frustrating moments to give me good advice. I know he loves me as though I am part of his family. He then began to sing a little louder, and soon everyone in the living room had drawn together and joined in to sing along. I will never forget the words to that song. He told me later it was a gospel tune that Kirk Franklin had written. No one recognized it by its name at the time, but everyone knew the words. Some people were still praying quietly, but above everything you could hear Coach Pops's voice confidently singing, "*He loves me and He cares, And He'll never put more on me than I can bear. . . .*" Those words seemed to connect all of us together. I remember the hope I felt as he put his hand on my head and sang those words over me.

I had been through so much adversity, and people would often say encouraging words like this to me—saying how God wouldn't give me anything I couldn't handle. But in that moment, I realized for the first time what the words to that song meant. It wasn't that God would keep us from a diagnosis or any other situation that could crush us, but it meant that He's always there to somehow get us through it. I looked around the room and realized that these were God's people. I didn't feel like I had to bear this on my own. The people with me singing that song and praying were the ones who were going to help me. God didn't stop Marfan syndrome from ending my career, but you can't tell me that He had not carefully planned the love and support I needed that night in the living room. He had brought together just the family I needed to bear this heartbreaking diagnosis.

As Coach Pops finished singing and his voice trailed off, I put my face in my shirt for a minute to fight back tears. Not tears of grief, but tears of joy for God's presence in my life, as well as for the support of my family all around me, including friends and players and coaches. There was a short minute of silence before Coach Pops began to speak. He began to preach to me what God was putting on his heart in that moment:

When I get weak, I trust Him. When I just don't know, I trust Him. When I can't figure it out, I trust Him. When I am on the mountaintop, I trust Him. When I am in the valley, I trust Him.

There were "Amen"s coming from around the room. But none of them were as loud as what I was hearing in my heart. *Trust* was the theme of my life. I had no answers, but I remembered Mom telling me that faith is the easy part—trust is where the real work begins. And then Coach Pops began to speak the words that changed my life. He spoke for several minutes, and the power of each word seemed to cover the quiet room with an unbelievable peace. He placed his hands on my shoulders and began to pray over me. Some of my family gathered around and placed their hands on his shoulders. I wasn't crying at that point, I was just there in the moment, open to whatever was going to happen next. Coach Pops prayed, "Lord, Isaiah has lost his dream. Help him to find a new way; help him to find new dreams. Lord, help Isaiah to dream again." Of all the prayers this man had prayed for me over the years, these words were the most powerful that anyone had ever spoken into my life. "God, help me dream again," I prayed.

It isn't that I could fully understand what God was doing at that moment. And to tell you the truth, I still can't completely see what it means for my life today, but I was able to get up from the stairs, and while the grief was still very present, I knew I needed to start taking steps to move on. Whatever *dreaming again* meant for me, it began where all my dreams had started: with my family. I needed to spend time with the people who had come together for me in that room, so I got up and began talking to my coaches and the people who were there to help me dream again. I needed to tell everyone how thankful I was for each of them in my life. Several minutes later, Mom's phone rang. It was Dr. Bonow from Northwestern and he wanted to speak with me. Mom talked with him for a minute and asked him if we could put him on the speakerphone. Everyone in our family wanted to hear what he had to say.

Looking back, this conversation with the doctor was the first moment where I actually saw what God had done. Dr. Bonow explained the situation to everyone and how the results had come back positive. He said that I should be very grateful for the diagnosis. It was hard to hear at first that I should be thankful for something that was taking my dream away. But he explained that this discovery had actually saved my life. If they hadn't identified the problem through the blood work and with the aortic enlargement in my heart, I could've easily died playing basketball. This diagnosis was saving my life.

We had a lot of conversations that night about well-known heart-related tragedies that had taken place on the basketball court. We talked about how blessed I had been to compete at an elite level and not have something terrible go wrong with my heart, especially a heart that was affected by this strange disease. I remember Coach Ray telling me that he was so thankful that nothing had ever happened to me as I was running one of his thousands of sprints. I started to realize how serious the diagnosis was, and while it didn't make losing basketball any easier, I started to realize how God had actually saved my life. It would be long after that evening when I would make even bigger connections about what God had done for me.

I was overwhelmed with the love in the room that night. After an hour or so, the coaches began to leave to get back to their families. Pastor Wible, who had driven up from Waco, prayed with me. Pastor Goines prayed with me, too. Coach Ray and I had a couple of moments together as well; he had been with me from the beginning and had been as excited as I was to see me walk across the stage on draft night, so I knew he was taking the news really hard, too. He knew the days ahead were going to be really tough for me, but since his goal had always been to make me a better man first before training me to be a great player, he was confident everything would turn out all right.

When my agent, Dwon, told me that he was working on what we were going to do next, I was a little confused. Dwon was an NBA agent. Now that I couldn't play, I had assumed that I wasn't someone he could work with. In my mind, it wasn't worth his time financially if I wasn't going to play. But he didn't see it that way at all; he wasn't concerned about the money. He told me as he left, "I am your agent, and I am not in this for your basketball career, I am in this for you." He said it was time for us to think about what we were going to do together next. It meant a lot to me.

Coach Drew spoke to my parents, saying that he had already made arrangements to keep me on scholarship at Baylor if it was something I was interested in doing. He wanted me to go back and get my degree and said that he and the rest of the coaching staff would be honored if I would hang around the program and help them out. He asked if I would be interested in being a student coach who could help mentor the younger guys. I realized that as soon as he received the bad news on Friday, his first concern was that I would be able to finish my degree. Coach Drew is always working to find the positives in any situation. It meant a lot to me that he had taken care of that before he even showed up at our house.

Later that evening, Cory Jefferson stopped in to see me. He had to drive a long way over to check in, and I knew he was getting ready for his workouts in New York City with the Knicks and the Nets in the next few days. He and I took a walk around the neighborhood and talked about everything we had been through that season. He was actually able to make me laugh, and it was good to get my mind off what had just happened, even if only for a couple of minutes. I asked him how he was feeling about the draft, and he said he felt good. It wasn't a heavy conversation or anything, but he was really upset about what had happened to me. Cory had always worn number 34, but he told me that he wanted to change his number to mine when he played in the league. He said he was going to go out there to play for both of us and he would carry the number 21 out there for me. I couldn't believe he would do that for me, because keeping the number you've played with for years is a big deal to athletes. I felt both honored and humbled by his words.

That night felt like the longest night of my life. If I didn't know any better, I would have believed that time had stood still or at least went in slow motion. Mom told me that Holly Rowe was coming to Dallas the next morning, and we would be taping an interview to share my story with ESPN. I stayed at Aunt Evelyn's house, and I remember that my parents' phones were going off late into the evening with reporters calling to get the story.

Word was leaking out about what had happened, but it was mainly local media. My Baylor guys and my family from Grace Prep were also slowly starting to find out, and they were all reaching out to me and sending encouraging texts.

THE NEXT MORNING I would be able to share my story on a national stage. I didn't think much about it. I couldn't. It was all really fresh. Late into the evening, after everyone had left and it was just my close family, we sat around Evelyn's house like we had done hundreds of times and talked. I don't know how my parents stayed awake after driving all night the evening before from Kansas City, but they still sat up with me for a long time.

I couldn't sleep soundly that night. Every time I woke up, the reality of the news would hit me. It was like getting hit in the foyer over and over again, because my mind would have to get readjusted to my new reality. I would get up and walk around for a minute and then try to sleep again. I was starting to have so many new questions. Was there a way to fix this problem with my heart so I could play? They had said I could never play again, but I was still really young. What if the doctors found a new treatment? How was Marfan going to affect my everyday life? Could I still work out? Could I stand to be around the sport I loved and not be able to play? Did my diagnosis mean I wouldn't live a long life? It seemed like there were new questions and so many things running through my mind.

When I woke up the next morning, we went straight to the Mo Williams Academy. I had taken the court there the previous day as I prepared for my Sunday workout in Chicago. Now there would be no Chicago trip. When life changes so quickly like that, it's hard to get your mind around what is actually happening, and everything kept playing in my mind over and over again. It was terribly difficult to gather my emotions and gain strength to even walk into that gym again. I had put in thousands of hours there to chase my dream. When I stepped on the court to meet with Holly, the emotions started to weigh me down, and I wasn't sure how I could do the ESPN interview.

I had a feeling it was always going to be hard for me to walk on the court from now on, but I needed to press on.

My family had lifted me up on Saturday night, but now I had to start doing the real work. I had been through this before. First you have to see your vision, and not until then can the real work begin. I am a competitor. I have to fight. I needed to have something to go after. My first thoughts that morning were positive, but I was still angry. I wanted to attack this disease. I wanted to bring awareness to it and beat it. That was my mind-set, even if it still meant I would never play basketball again. Maybe by doing the interview, it could somehow make a difference.

Since Holly is a family friend, we took a few moments to talk before the interview, and she said she knew it was going to be hard for both of us. It was one of the most difficult conversations I've ever had—and it happened for an interview that would be seen all over the world. Since I hadn't slept well, my emotions kept rushing in and taking over when I tried to talk. By the time we started taping, it was all I could do just to get in front of the camera. When I finally sat down and Holly asked me what had happened, I was able to pull it together for just long enough. I explained the situation and the danger of my arteries being enlarged by Marfan syndrome. And then I got to that word. I tripped into it, because it was a word I had used my whole life. I said, "I had a *dream* that my name was going to be called—" And then the truth of everything that had happened in the past day floored me again, nearly as hard as it had in the foyer at Aunt Evelyn's house. I tried to get myself together. I knew it was emotional for Holly and I didn't want to cry on national television.

That word, though—"dream"—had driven me my whole life. When it slipped out, the fact that I would never walk across that stage on NBA draft night was too much for me to deal with. Fortunately, I was able to gather myself and Holly helped me out with another question. Of all the people in the world who could've been interviewing me at that moment, I was so thankful it was her. I apologized to my fans, who would never get to see me play, and told the camera that it wasn't the end for me, only the beginning.

And that wasn't me trying to say all the right things. I wanted this not to be the end, but a real beginning for something greater. I just didn't know what that meant for me.

We taped the interview early and it ran on ESPN later that morning. I haven't watched the interview yet and don't know if I will anytime soon because my emotions were so raw. It captured the moment of my pain—the real grief I was feeling just hours after finding out. My dream had been so much a part of who I was, and now I was feeling so empty.

We hung around the gym that day for a while. There were so many people who wanted to interview me, but I couldn't do them all. Mo had kids coming in for workouts that afternoon, so I spent the rest of the day staying busy by working with the kids. Helping them get better was a great distraction from everything going on.

Eventually my family and Evelyn and Dre's family were able to go out to eat together. Being around them was great, because it also allowed me to focus on other things besides my bad news. I would spend the rest of the week hanging out with them at my aunt and uncle's house when I wasn't doing media or planning my next step with Dwon. I've never been so thankful to be around people who have so much joy in their house no matter the situation. The news was out. I still had no idea what was coming next, but things were starting to get interesting.

Coaches, teachers, and pastors talk about moving on. On the

basketball court we call it a "next play" mentality. The thing about the next play is that it starts as a state of mind. Moving on to the next play doesn't erase the last one. It just means that you are going to move forward and focus on what's in front of you. The news from that Saturday night would hurt me for months, but I had to move on to the next play. I couldn't sit there and feel sorry for what had happened. That week I received so much love from Baylor nation that it was unbelievable. I received encouraging messages from guys in the league who I had never even met. As hard as it was, I was overwhelmed at times with how many people reached out in support. And that week I also started to understand more about the miracle that had occurred in my life with this diagnosis.

CHAPTER 10

GOD'S PLAN

From the moment Coach Pops preached his "dream again" in the living room at Aunt Evelyn's house, I was waiting for God to actually answer. I knew Coach was right, but I also knew that it was going to be tough to trust that God had a plan after all this. The thing I've learned through a life of overcoming difficulty is that waiting for God to answer doesn't mean you sit around and do nothing. You need to pick yourself up, move forward, and try to focus on what you can do for other people. I had always known that one day the ball would stop bouncing. I just didn't think it would happen as quickly and as soon as it did. I was hoping to find out what God's new plan for my life looked like.

I jumped right back into work the night before, getting out there on the court with the kids at Mo's Academy. There were moments by myself when stuff was hard to deal with, but I tried to keep busy by lifting other people up. One of the things my family has always taught me is that the best way to work through a problem is to focus on helping other people—to look outside yourself for someone you can help. My mom has always said that's what it means to love other people. She would quote 1 John 4:8 to me: *"Whoever does not know love does not know God, because God is love."* I even have that verse tattooed on my wrist because it is so important to me. This was my opportunity to love other people.

After the news broke nationally with the ESPN interview, the outpouring of support was so huge it made my head spin. I had guys like Charles Barkley, Kenny Smith, Deion Sanders, and so many others reach out to offer their support. At this point, there were only a few moments left for me to try to process everything that had happened. Coach Drew would say that "character is revealed in tough times," and I was focused on letting my real character come through. It was okay to have weak moments and I did when I was by myself. I had lost everything except my faith and my family and I was holding on tight to both those things. Knowing I had a family that loved me and a faith that was lifting me up and helping me walk forward through all this kept me focused on what I could do to help other people. When Monday came along, it seemed like God started to slowly show me what He was up to.

Monday morning was busy. I had an interview with Fox Sports about my story that would run nationally. I began to think about the people who might have this syndrome but didn't have the NBA combine to discover it. I wanted to raise awareness about the disease in hopes that someone's life might be saved by hearing my story. I kept thinking about a young kid like me out there playing who had no idea he or she had Marfan syndrome.

Dwon called me early that morning to tell me I should expect to be contacted by the NBA commissioner. He had spoken with Chrysa Chin and Ned Cohen, who both worked for the league's front office, and they had invited me to attend the draft as the commissioner's honorary guest. It was one more act of kindness that made me feel thankful. Since the terrible news on Saturday night, I had envisioned watching the draft on television with my family, but when Dwon told me I was still invited, my first thought was that I would have the chance to go and support so many of my dudes who would have their moment that Thursday night. It was going to be a great night for so many of the people I cared about, and I felt honored to be invited. I got an e-mail later that day from Commissioner Adam Silver, who extended the invitation to my family, Dwon, and Coach Ray to attend the draft at the Barclays Center in Brooklyn, New York, and to participate in all of the predraft events. The e-mail also explained that he wanted to honor me during the evening in some way, but he didn't provide any specifics. Even after all my dreaming, I still wasn't in a place to imagine what would happen next.

THE NEXT SEVERAL days were off-the-hook busy as I did local interviews with different Dallas-area reporters explaining my situation. The story had gotten a little bit of national attention, but it was still more of a Texas story. When I wasn't doing interviews, I was with my family. They were really holding me up through all the emotions and busyness of the week.

In those few days, I also started to realize that I couldn't take basketball out of my life. It was my passion, and I couldn't totally walk away from it. Coach Drew had talked about my helping out with the Baylor program and working with the guys. I had jumped right back into coaching the kids at Mo's Academy on Sunday night, and it felt good to be on the floor and to help kids improve. I began to get my mind around going back to Baylor. If I couldn't play in the NBA, the Baylor family was who I wanted to be with. Every single one of the coaches would text me each day to check on me. Sometimes it was to ask how I was doing, some days it was an inspirational quote or a Bible verse. They always had my back. The more I thought about it, the more pleased I was that I could go back home to Waco in the fall and be around my team and friends. I wasn't sure that being a coach was a good look for me, but I wanted to stay involved in the game somehow.

I still couldn't get Coach Pops's words out of my head from that Saturday night as I realized they had become my own prayer. In fact, I made it the theme for the T-shirts we were having printed up. It was my image with my trademark glasses set in Baylor colors, and it read DREAM AGAIN really big across the front. I kept praying that God would follow through and help me to dream again. I was always driven by my dream of playing in the NBA, but that dream had also included doing work off the court that would help other people. Dwon and I began to imagine how we could help other people live out the words in Coach Pops's prayer . . . how could we help other people dream again?

Dwon and I had already started working on a website and set in motion all that needed to happen to form a foundation to raise money for Marfan syndrome research. Dwon was working on what it would look like for us to raise as much money as we could. Beyond that specific disease, I wanted to share hope with people who were faced with their own impossible situations, no matter what form they took. We all wanted to turn my bad news into as many pluses for other people as we possibly could.

I was also beginning to learn more about the disease that had taken my career from me. We were still looking at the possibility of surgeries or treatments that would allow me to play, but nothing looked promising. I felt hopeful that I could team up with others to get involved in helping to raise awareness. We were leaving for New York in just a day, and Dwon was able to set up a meeting with Carolyn Levering, the CEO of the Marfan Foundation.

After three short days packed with interviews, spending the rest of my time around the Academy working with the kids, and hanging out with Aunt Evelyn and my family, it was time to fly to New York for the draft. I was humbled that Commissioner Silver had asked me to come to the draft, and even more thrilled that he also invited my family. I was excited to see my college teammate Cory, and my high school AAU teammate and good friend Marcus, have their night. Basketball is a fraternity. From the time you are young you get to know the other elite players in the country and you get close to them. Cory and I had become like brothers in the past year, and Marcus and I had been close since junior high. It was going to be a proud moment for me when those two were selected. I knew many of the guys in my draft class well and was excited that I could be there when they made their way across that stage and into the league. I knew what it took to get your name called that night, and each of those guys deserved all the respect in the world. Just because my dream was gone didn't mean I couldn't celebrate the dreams these guys had worked for their whole lives.

We flew out of Dallas early in the morning, and after arriving in New York City, I rushed over to NBC studios to tape an appearance on a show called *SportsDash*. I tried to be as honest as I could possibly be with the interviewers. I said I was excited to see the guys in that draft class walk across the stage. When they asked me what was next, I told them that I hoped God would unravel that for me a little bit faster, but for now I was focused on trying to bring some hope to others by the way I handled my situation.

After the interview, we were taken to the various gifting suites at the hotel. This was another humbling experience for me. All of the athletes who participate on draft night are showered with gifts from different sponsors. I got to visit the suites set up by Foot Locker, Beats by Dr. Dre, and others, where they showered me with gifts as if I were an NBA draftee. They were treating me like everyone else who was going to be invited into the league the following evening. I will never forget the first-class treatment the NBA and all of those companies showed me.

Later that night, we went to meet with Carolyn Levering to discuss ways that we could bring more awareness to the disease.

At this point in my journey, I was still in the early stages of understanding the disease and what it would mean for me long-term. I still had a lot of questions. I had been talking with my parents in those past couple of days about what might have been if I had never been flagged at the combine. What if I hadn't declared for the draft? What if I had gone back to Baylor and played? It was a slow process, but I was beginning to see the evidence of God working through this whole situation. As Carolyn and I met, it was as if God were opening a door and beginning to reveal the next step in His plan for me, even my next dream. Marfan syndrome is very rare, and we talked about all the ways that I could help raise money and bring hope to people around the world with whom I shared this disease.

I had always been part of a team working toward a single cause. As we met with Carolyn that night, I started to realize that I was joining a new team with a purpose much greater than winning basketball games. We were working to save people's lives. She invited me to Baltimore, where they were hosting an opportunity for people who had Marfan syndrome to gather and meet and talk about the disease and how it affects their lives. She said it would be great for me to talk with others who could understand what I was going through. Even with all the cool opportunities I experienced that day, the meeting and planning about the foundation brought more hope into my situation. I returned to the hotel with my family early that night. The next morning

Mom and I would tape a national television show together for the first time since the ESPN special.

I WOKE UP early, not realizing everything that God had planned for the day. We were out of the hotel early and went over to the *Good Morning America* studios to meet Robin Roberts and the whole crew there. Robin was so cool. She had been a player in her day and so we connected right away. She had seen her own fair share of adversity, too, having battled cancer like my aunt Evelyn. In person, when the cameras are off, Robin is exactly the same as she is on television—genuine and nice.

We were taping an interview that would run on their national show later that week. I had been on plenty of interviews in the past week on my own, but when we sat down to tape, I was excited for everyone to hear my mom, the person who had inspired me all of my life, share words about her faith.

Robin asked how we were dealing with the situation, and Mom shared with her the words that had inspired me as a young man when I was dealing with my eye surgeries. She told Robin that I could make it my excuse or I could make it my story. I was able to explain my hope to inspire people who were facing big challenges to hang on to their dreams and to fight for them. I told her that my faith and my family had helped me to face the challenges that life had brought my way. I was hoping to share with others the importance of staying positive and getting on your knees to pray when things got tough. I was talking to the camera, but I was also reminding myself of those same things.

When we left the studio that morning, there was only one thought in my mind: today was draft day. It was the day I had worked for and dreamed about my entire life. Since my arrival in New York, I had been so busy that I hadn't slowed down enough to reflect on what that night meant. But when I walked into Barclays Center with Dwon, Coach Ray, and my family, I was both overwhelmed and thrilled beyond belief. We were treated like every other member of the draft class and were given a suite and then seated at a table on the floor. It was my first time sitting in the crowd watching the big event that I had worked so hard for since I was a five-year-old kid in Fresno. I focused on celebrating the guys who were drafted and was hopeful that the evening would go well for my closest friends.

About a half hour into the draft, right after the fifteenth pick, something happened that would humble me forever. The Atlanta Hawks had just selected Adreian Payne, a good player from Michigan State, when Adam Silver came to the microphone again. He paused for a moment and then said, "Before we continue tonight, I want to take a moment to recognize Baylor center Isaiah Austin." This was the moment they had told me about. It was the moment they were going to honor me. I stood up from the table and waved, and the crowd began to cheer. He continued:

> *You may have heard about Isaiah. He's one of the nation's best collegiate players and was expected to be picked tonight before the discovery, just a few days ago, that he had a genetic disorder called Marfan syndrome and is no longer able to play competitive basketball. But like the other young men here tonight, Isaiah dedicated himself through endless hard work and dedication to a potential career as a professional basketball player, and we wanted to make sure he fulfilled at least this part of his dream . . .*

When Adam Silver said the word "dream," it was like the whole world slowed down for just a second. I was standing and still waving to the crowd, but I began to realize what the commissioner was about to do . . . and I was completely overcome with emotion. My family and Dwon stood up at the table alongside me; I realized that they had known all about this. Then Commissioner Silver said:

> *So it gives me great pleasure to say that with the next pick in the 2014 NBA draft, the NBA selects Isaiah Austin from Baylor University.*

All of my life it had been my dream to walk across that stage on draft night. So many people had shared that vision with me. It was a lifetime of prayers, hard work, and trust—even when things looked really tough. For my entire life, up until the moment I received that terrible news on June 21, I believed that God had given me that dream; I knew it would come true. But just five days earlier I thought it was over. I had assumed that Marfan syndrome had taken it from me forever, but God had a better plan. He always does. There are moments when you feel God's presence around you, and then there are moments when you actually see Him doing His work. This was God's work in action.

At Adam Silver's words, I began to make my way to the platform. I was stunned when I realized that this was the moment God had promised when he planted the dream in my heart. The crowd was on its feet, giving me a standing ovation, cheering me on loudly. My family had tears of joy in their eyes. In Coach Ray's and Dwon's eyes I could see how proud they were of me. My friends around the room were giving me so much love as I approached the stage. That moment it hit me: when God plants a dream in your heart, when God makes a promise to you, nothing can stop Him from delivering. I wanted to stay composed as I made that walk to the stage, but it was difficult. I had two thoughts—I didn't want to cry, and I didn't want to trip walking up onto the stage.

You could say that things didn't happen exactly the way I had planned, but after all those years of working, trusting, and dreaming, it didn't matter to me in that moment. All I could think about was that I was finally there. It looked just like I had always thought it would be in my vision: *I was dressed in a crisp suit, sitting at a table with my family, hugging my mom and dad when my name was called, walking up those stairs to shake hands with the commissioner, taking the franchise hat, smiling for the cameras . . .*

It was honorary, but it felt like a miracle. God had restored the dream that I believed Marfan syndrome had crushed five days earlier, and He made it come true for the whole world to see. Isn't that cool about God? The Bible says in Ephesians 3:20, He *"is able to do immeasurably more than all we ask or imagine, according to His power that is at work within us."*

When I was onstage with the commissioner, I kept thanking him. I had never been so thankful to anyone in my life. When he leaned over to put his arm around me for the cameras, he said, "Isaiah, you are part of the NBA family now." He couldn't have known how much those words meant to me. I don't know if he understood how much the word "family" meant to me. I stood there on the stage and was able to appreciate what was happening. I had wanted a franchise hat, but I was given something much bigger and longer lasting than that. It wasn't a hat with the logo of the Celtics or the Bulls or the Clippers or the Spurs. It was a symbol of my being drafted into the NBA *family*. My dream as a kid had still somehow come true. But I was also very aware in that moment that I was being drafted into a cause much bigger than playing basketball. I was being given the chance to have an opportunity and a voice to impact people on a bigger stage than I ever could've imagined.

When any NBA draftee walks off that stage, he's immediately thrown into interviews. I was able to talk with Jay Williams of ESPN right after I came down those stairs and was able to share my outlook on what had happened. I was overwhelmed with thankfulness in those moments. Sure, my postdraft interviews weren't exactly what I had always imagined they would be like, having the opportunity to talk about how I was going to help the franchise that had selected me get better and win multiple championships. I had always pictured myself talking about my skills as a stretch five and my intention to work as hard as I could to be a great team player. I had always imagined talking about me. Instead I was talking about my faith. I was talking about God. I was challenging people who were discouraged by life to find ways to dream again.

I've heard people say that my honorary draft moment was the best moment of the evening. It sure was for my family and me. Many of my friends participating in the draft had great nights, too. The Celtics drafted Marcus Smart, and Cory Jefferson was drafted by the Spurs but then traded to the Nets. I couldn't have been happier for those guys. After the interviews I went back to the suite with my family, Ray, and Dwon. Later, while everyone was having their draft parties, I went out with my family. Mom, Dad, Noah, and Narah would have to get back to Kansas City soon, while I was going back to Dallas to discover my next steps. We walked around the city for a bit and ate dinner at an Italian restaurant. Nothing crazy; we were just celebrating like we do—as a family. It was a night I would remember for the rest of my life.

IN THE DAYS after the draft, my schedule began to pick up even more. While Coach Drew had offered my scholarship back, I had to figure out how I could get back into my classes so late in the game. I spent time refocusing on school and my major and what I needed to do in order to finish my degree. I had two more years of college ahead of me, and I was beginning to understand what my next move would be after basketball.

Even though not much time had passed since I learned of my diagnosis, I immediately wanted God to reveal what He had in store for me next. Yes, I was very impatient, but now that the draft was over, it was like God had me running an all-out sprint. There was a huge response to my *Good Morning America* interview as well as to my interviews with ESPN and the NBA from draft night. I had flown back to Dallas but was home for only a couple of days before I had to get things together and head to Los Angeles for what would become a month of traveling, speaking, and doing interviews. Mom and Dwon said I was building a platform to encourage other people. Whatever God was up to, He was definitely giving me the chance to share my faith and inspire millions of people.

The next few weeks proved to be God working to unfold His next steps for me. It was so fast-paced that I couldn't clearly see everything He was doing in my life. I still had difficult moments when it would hit me like a ton of bricks that basketball had been taken away from me. But there were still moments when I started to imagine somehow playing again.

As July began, I traveled with Dwon to Baltimore for the Marfan conference that Carolyn had invited me to. It wasn't a speaking engagement; it was a conference that gathered people from around the country who had the disease. It was truly inspiring. During the conference the organizers split up the attendees by specific age groups. There were some seminars, but it was mainly a lot of social events. It was great, because I had the time to connect with people my age and talk with them about their own experiences. We went out to dinners, went on a day cruise, and did a lot of fun activities that gave us space to relax and hang out. I made a new friend named Michelle there, who was really outgoing, and she quickly connected me with her circle of friends—a group of people who I still reach out to for support. The Baltimore trip allowed me to spend time with people who had learned how to live with this condition. But I was still discovering a lot about my diagnosis.

I quickly learned that Marfan syndrome affects people from *all* walks of life and all different backgrounds. I met young kids, ages eight to ten, who, like me, had been recently diagnosed. It was good for me to spend time with them and talk to their parents. I was inspired by the courage and toughness of those kids. They were in the same place I was, learning to see the diagnosis as a blessing—something that had saved our lives.

There were parts of the conference experience that freaked me out a little bit. I talked with people who had gone through the aorta-replacement surgery that my doctors were saying I might need someday. It wasn't the heart thing that bothered me as much as the surgery thing, because of my eye operations. The thought of having to go through another surgery shook me up.

I left my first conference in Baltimore having made new friends who would remain a big part of my support system. The conference also got me thinking about how important it was for people with Marfan syndrome to be diagnosed so they could get the proper treatment. Awareness is a big deal, and I started talking more with Dwon about figuring out ways that we could bring attention to the disease and make an impact in people's lives. I left Baltimore thinking about those brave kids and wondering about the ones out there who weren't lucky enough to be diagnosed and treated by a doctor. That trip, in many ways, grounded me for the things that were ahead.

Next I flew from Baltimore to Las Vegas for the NBA's summer league. My new NBA family invited me to participate as an intern with the NBA TV live broadcasts of the summer league games they held each preseason. They let me do some player analysis and fun interviews talking ball with the guys who were in the summer program. I was then asked to do some broadcasting on the red carpet at ESPN's awards program, the ESPYS, which gave me the chance to bring even more exposure to Marfan syndrome. After the ESPYS, they throw an after-party for everyone who attends, and I was able to hang out with so many great people who I admire, like Drake, Lolo Jones, Kevin Durant, Michael Westbrook, Andre Drummond, and Blake Griffin. I had already known Kevin for a couple of years because I had attended his camps, and he had been supportive about what I was going through. Everyone was really encouraging. I spent some time talking with Carmelo Anthony that night, and he said something that still means a lot to me today. He told me that I was one of the guys in the draft who he thought was going to be a great player in the league. It was a cool thing to hear from a guy who had always been one of my favorite professional players.

I had been named the official spokesperson of the Marfan Foundation, so everywhere I traveled I was aware that I was carrying the banner for awareness about the disease. I did a number of national interviews throughout that busy time. I was even invited to talk with Larry King in Los Angeles and it was a really good interview. I was there for three or four hours, and for an eighty-one-year-old, Mr. King is one of the most energetic guys you could ever be around. He's the type of guy who comes in and makes sure he stops to talk to everyone in the room. Throughout these events, I started to realize how much I enjoyed broadcasting. While I was set on returning to Baylor to finish my degree, there were a lot of moments when I thought about how comfortable and at home I felt on camera and around the microphone. God was showing me where my next steps might be if I couldn't play the game I loved.

The most memorable moment for me in those days was definitely my visit to the White House. I was able to handle *Good Morning America*, the red carpet at the ESPYS, NBA television, and even Larry King with no sweat. None of that stuff even made me nervous, but when Dwon and I traveled to DC, and I knew I was going to meet the president of the United States . . . man, I got to tell you, that's the kind of thing that will make you nervous! It was at the end of a fourteen-day run of events, and I also think it was the first moment I had a chance to sit back and reflect on the crazy stuff that had happened in my life since my diagnosis.

I was never really worried about how my suit looked when I did these other events, but I might have pressed my shirt nearly fifteen times before Dwon and I left the hotel to go the White House. I actually asked Dwon to help me with my shirt because I didn't want wrinkles in it, and he laughed and said I was reminding him of a kid going to his first day of school. It was so humbling to get invited to meet the president. I was attending with a group of athletes and some other NBA people. Chris Paul and Roger Mason were both in the group.

President Obama shook my hand and said he admired the way I had handled my situation. I thanked him for inviting me there and told him how much it meant for Marfan syndrome awareness. There are only a handful of people who ever get the chance to shake hands with the American president, and I was now on that list. And the fact that the president knew who I was and said he was inspired by my story was something I will never forget. He also invited me back to the White House to shoot baskets with him sometime.

As my postdraft travels came to a close and I began to think back to June 21, I realized how much I had learned about how God works. I had my one dream my whole life. My plan was to walk across the stage on draft night and join an NBA team. Some days I feel my dream wasn't big enough for God. He stepped in and not only made my dream come true in a way that I could never have imagined, but He brought me to platforms, stages, and microphones that I would never have experienced had I not been diagnosed with Marfan syndrome. I learned that God's plan is always about helping people find ways to dream again.

CHAPTER 11

DREAMING AGAIN

By now you know that my vision will always be a big deal to me. When I talk about my vision today, though, I am talking about more than just my eyesight and what pushed me toward the NBA. I realize I've been lifted up my entire life by the people I call family and steadied by my faith in God.

There isn't a day that goes by that I don't miss competing on the court. Basketball has always been everything to me, and I don't believe I will ever be able to completely walk away from it. Whenever I walk through the mall or even stop to put gas in my car, people always say something about my height and usually follow it up with a comment like, "I hope you play basketball." I will keep getting better at saying, "No, but I used to."

I've realized that my story is more about dreams than it is about a sport. And I wouldn't have it any other way. Right now, I am putting in the work it takes to dream again. Every dream has its own obstacles. Everything worth dreaming about takes the same kind of work that I put into getting me in a position to be drafted in the NBA. I've realized that the difficult things I've had to go through have put me in a situation to encourage others to never stop dreaming. And I am thankful for that.

I went back to Baylor in the fall following the draft and jumped into my responsibilities with school and with the basketball program. It was different at first, getting back into the rhythm of doing classes, mainly because I thought I would be starting a job this fall. I spent all my life thinking I would be starting an NBA career at this point in my life. It was another adjustment I had to make. School has always been a priority to me, but before my diagnosis I was studying for a degree I would use "someday" after my basketball career. I enjoy my marketing and business classes and having some more time to meet people and experience campus life.

My role with the Baylor basketball team is a lot different

now. Sometimes it's still hard not to be out there on the court playing with those guys. There are moments when it hurts. But I also think it has been good for me to stay so close to the game I love: it is forcing me to come to terms with my new relationship with basketball. And because I am now removed from the competition, I am learning to see the game differently. I try to get guys up to the gym early to put in the work necessary to be great. I am mainly focused on helping other guys be successful on the court. I try to encourage them and give advice about how to handle the pressures that go along with playing ball at this level. At practice I used to dunk and rain threes; now I officiate scrimmages, wipe up sweat from the floor, and bring water to the guys on break. I do the same things I've watched Coach Drew and the other Baylor coaches do every day for years.

I hope that I can help the program do something special while I am here finishing up my degree. I've gotten to know the coaches on a different level now that I am not a player, and that's pretty cool. I'm learning a lot about coaching, faith, and being a servant leader from those guys. I know it might always be hard on me to watch the game, unable to be out there competing in it. I am trying to focus my competitive energy into finishing school and moving on to what God has for me next. Baylor University and Baylor basketball will always be my family. It will always be a special place for me.

These last few months I have had people tell me that I am

good on camera and with the media and that I should consider broadcasting someday. As much fun as I have had being on television with Larry King, NBA TV, or interviewing people on the red carpet at the ESPYS, I am pretty convinced right now that that is not the path I will take. I have been offered a job with the National Basketball Association when I graduate from Baylor. Working for the league in some capacity, most likely through the NBA Cares program, is a great opportunity and will definitely be my first career step. I am grateful to Adam Silver and the NBA for that offer and their support. Even though I can no longer play at a competitive level, my love for the game still continues to grow. I think at some point in my career I might want to pursue coaching as a full-time job. I love the opportunity to motivate and inspire people (it is one of the things I love so much about my speaking opportunities around the country), and coaching gives you the chance to do that for people. I watch my Baylor guys like Coach Drew, Coach Mac, Coach Maloney, Coach Nuness, and Coach Mills, and my high school mentor Coach Ray make a huge impact on young men each and every day. So maybe I'll be coaching ten years from now? Who knows? I have a long way to go. I can only imagine that my love for the game will never go away.

Just like basketball will always be part of my life, I know that Marfan syndrome will, too. I've learned so much about my illness from the Marfan Foundation, and my trip to the Marfan conference in Baltimore that summer (they call it the "Mar-family") helped me find people like my friend Michelle, who I can call up and ask for advice. It is a group of people who can relate to my situation because they are in it, too. I am also thankful for the opportunity to encourage other people who are dealing with the disease.

I recently made friends with this guy Carson. He and I have a lot in common because he loves basketball as much as I do and he is also dealing with a relatively new Marfan syndrome diagnosis. Carson is ten years old and lives in the Waco area. I always laugh about the first time I came over to his house to hang out with him, because he let me in the door without telling me he had the biggest dog I had ever seen in my life! When the dog came charging around the corner to greet me there was a second or two when I thought a bear had broken into his house. It was a pretty funny moment.

Carson is one of the strongest kids I have ever met, and his courage has been a real blessing and inspiration to me. He hasn't allowed Marfan syndrome to change him. He's a true fighter and hasn't backed down. I always tell him that we are going to stay positive and make it through these challenges together. Carson and I text back and forth some; we play video games and go out to hit a round of golf when I am not busy traveling the country. He's a tough dude who encourages me every bit as much as I hope to encourage him.

Marfan syndrome is a big part of my story and I want you to understand a little bit about the disease. There are a lot of misconceptions about the illness. First off, there are actually people who think Marfan syndrome has something to do with a person's intelligence. That is a really big misunderstanding and one that sets me off sometimes. Some of the smartest, most talented people I have met deal with the syndrome. Let me start from the beginning and tell you a little about what I've learned these last few months. Marfan is named after the French doctor who discovered the disease in 1896. The syndrome attacks your body's connective tissue (connective tissue, by the way, is found *everywhere* in your body); it is what holds all of the body's cells and organs together. But that connective tissue also plays an important role in helping the body grow and develop. It's probably one of the reasons Coach Charlie (my good friend, otherwise known as "the Punisher") and my other trainers could never get me to bulk up and put on extra weight while I was playing. One of the common symptoms is that people with the condition have a low body muscle mass and a very small amount of body fat. Marfan is caused by a genetic mutation (found in chromosome 15) that affects the way your body produces a protein called TGF beta. The increase in that protein is what causes problems.

The syndrome affects the heart, blood vessels, bones, joints, and, yes, even eyes. It actually affects the way you grow, too, so many people with it happen to be really tall. Another one of the effects of Marfan can be life-threatening and it's one that I have. Marfan can cause a condition called aortic enlargement, which means that the main blood vessel that carries blood away from the heart to the rest of the body is bigger than it should be. Blood-pressure drugs can be effective in treating the symptoms of the disease, and heart surgery is often an option.

Marfan syndrome affects people of all ages and all races, about one out of every five thousand people in the United States. The doctors believe that three out of four people with Marfan syndrome have inherited it. The most dangerous thing about the disease is that it isn't easily detected. Some children are born with obvious signs of it, but for many people the symptoms don't develop fully until they get closer to their adult years. Sometimes I wonder if that is the reason I was flagged but then cleared of it when I was in junior high.

People have asked me if it ever hurts. But, thankfully, it doesn't hurt me. I am still learning about the different ways the disease affects me, but right now I am fortunate to be able to run, work out, and even play a little ball (*only* at a recreational pace). But the doctors say I am fortunate to be active, and it might have something to do with the way I have trained my body for all these years. To continue to push my body through the physicality and stress of elite-level play, though, could've been deadly for me. Right now, the doctors believe that at the rate the disease is advancing with me, I may not have to have heart surgery for ten to fifteen years. I hope that is true and I am keeping my fingers crossed that by then there will be new medicines to treat the condition without having to go through heart surgery. Maybe my fund-raising can play a part in solving that for me and the thousands of others affected in this way by the disease.

While my diagnosis is a *part* of my story, it's not the biggest part. I understand now some of the amazing things that God was doing in my life that none of us realized at the time. I'm thankful that God brought me into a family that would give me the kind of support I needed to survive what He knew I would have to face. I think about the experience of going through each eye surgery, praying that I would get my vision back, and then having my hopes crushed each time it didn't work out. I wonder how I would've handled that devastating news on June 21 if I hadn't already gone through each one of those terrible operations and learned to handle disappointment.

God helped train me to handle adversity by dealing with my blindness all those years on the court. I had to learn how to trust Him. I've since learned that many Marfan syndrome patients deal with detached retinas. We didn't know it at the time, but it wasn't likely that any of the surgeries could have been successful. I am thankful that even with my "disability," I was still able to play basketball at a competitive level, and the doctors today tell me that may be why I've handled the disease so well. It has not slowed me down yet.

I am thankful for Mom and Ben, because each time I faced adversity with my eyesight I had to learn to fall back on the things they had taught me about my faith in God.

There are other great parts to the story that I've started to see more clearly. The 2014 draft combine was the first time the NBA put their players through the types of screening that we had to undergo. It was the first time I could've entered the draft and had my condition diagnosed. My torn labrum the year before seemed like a freak accident—it may or may not have had anything to do with my condition—but it might've saved my life by keeping me out of that year's draft. If I had gone into the draft after my freshman year like I had planned to do, my condition may never have been diagnosed. During my sophomore year I matured and embraced the Baylor family and found a support system with Coach Drew and those guys who have helped me since my diagnosis.

I've talked with the coaches about what might've happened to me on the practice floor or in a game at Baylor. It is a scary thought. But doctors have said that the NBA puts a different level of physical stress on your body. There is a level of physicality and speed when you're on the floor in the league that's a lot different from college.

I've begun to realize in these past few months how God worked through all of these situations to save my life. And after life delivered the toughest news, when I found out that I could never again play the sport I loved, God still delivered on my dream. It wasn't exactly the way I had always seen it in my vision, but I believe now that it was even better. It was a new version of my lifelong dream. God began to open doors for me that would never have been possible if things had gone the way I planned. And that brings me back to talking about dreams.

My story is about dreams and what it takes to make them come true. I've started the Isaiah Austin Foundation because of dreams. It came from a dark moment in my life that God turned into a positive. "Dreaming again" means that we should learn to accept the unexpected things that life throws our way. God has brought so many people into my life these past few years as I've learned to dream again. I've partnered with the Marfan Foundation. I am speaking whenever and wherever I can around the country to continue to raise awareness of the disease in hopes that people who don't know they have it can be diagnosed and treated. So many people have pitched in and helped with that process.

This past fall I have been really blessed by all the people who have supported my efforts to raise awareness for Marfan syndrome. On October 30, 2014, the Boston Celtics brought me to their home court, TD Garden, for their opening home game and presented me with a jersey. People diagnosed with Marfan syndrome were invited to the game, and the president of the Marfan Foundation, my friend John McGrath, attended. There were some really special moments at that event. First off, the Celts were playing my close friend and former Baylor teammate Cory Jefferson's squad, the Brooklyn Nets, and I got to see him play his first NBA minutes that night! Second, the Celtics presented me with my number, 21, which they actually had to bring out of retirement. Finally, the attention the evening brought to Marfan syndrome was priceless. That night was a big deal for me, a big deal for bringing awareness to Marfan syndrome, and one that I will never forget: I will be a Boston Celtic for life, another dream come true for me.

A few days before the Boston event, on October 24, Coach Drew, my Baylor family, the NBA, and the Dallas Mavericks worked together to help launch the Isaiah Austin Foundation's inaugural fund-raising event. It was held at American Airlines Arena in Dallas. We had a really nice dinner and an auction to raise money for Marfan research and awareness. I was humbled by the support everyone threw behind the event. It was an awesome night. Coach Drew and my Baylor family have responded by getting behind me in my efforts. Coach has been really supportive about my getting out in front of people to talk about Marfan awareness and research.

And just in case you were wondering, God didn't leave anything out when he delivered on my NBA dream. Since I was a kid, I always looked forward to seeing my face included in my favorite video game, NBA 2K. It's one of the things all the guys

I came up playing ball with dream about. In the fall, the EA sports people flew me to California and took some scans of my face so I could be included in the game. It was incredible to go behind the scenes at 2K games and see how everything gets done. I love to play video games, and being involved is one of those cool little extras about playing in the league. It was also a big deal to some of my fans and my friends like Carson, who are into the 2K games. I sat back and smiled when 2K made the announcement in December that players could now draft me onto their teams in the game. It was one more reminder to me that when God follows through, He pays attention to every little detail. I'm not gonna lie, either; I'm putting up some pretty good numbers right now in my own 2K franchise NBA career.

I read that my diagnosis and the attention it received back in June made a huge impact on the number of people who knew about the disease, and I plan to continue that trend with my work traveling the country and speaking to people about it. I am hoping to raise money to continue research so that someday a Marfan diagnosis might mean something different for the people who have the illness than it did for me.

But the other important part of what I am doing when I speak and raise money through my foundation is to give people some hope. I want to help people understand what a blessing life is and to try to be there to encourage others to find what it really means to dream again in their own lives. If you ask me what I will to be doing in fifteen years, I can tell you that no matter what it is, I hope I'm still encouraging and inspiring people. Right now, I spend many of my weekends traveling and speaking to groups, trying to do just that. I feel like I am one of the lucky ones, learning to find a new dream, and I want to bring that message to others.

So, like I have told you from the beginning: my vision is a huge deal to me. I don't ever take it for granted. I've always taken great pride in how well I saw the game of basketball, especially when I was out there competing on the court. And I've worked hard to see those things with one good eye better than most players could with two. But when I talk about the way "I see," I now talk about something much bigger.

"Life vision" is all about how well you can visualize your dreams. I've learned how to look toward the positive, to see my dreams coming true even when they took an unexpected turn. I want to share that with other people because I believe dreams are important. My dream is what drove me through all kinds of discouragement. Dreaming again has been God's gift to me, and I want to tell as many people about it as I possibly can.

Some people still ask me at my speaking engagements how I feel about my lifelong dream of being a professional basketball player not coming true. The truth is that I wouldn't trade my NBA dream for anything in the world, because it has made me who I am today. There are so many people out there who are afraid to go after their dreams, and the ones who do sometimes walk away from them when life crashes in on them and things become difficult or don't work out exactly the way they wanted. I want to encourage people to follow through and hang on to their visions.

The kind of dreaming I am talking about comes from hard work.

It comes from grinding it out every day, especially on the days when you don't feel like working.

It comes from the support of family, from learning to see each adversity as an opportunity.

It comes from filling your mind with positive thoughts even when everything in the world around you feels negative.

Like Joseph in the Bible—God gave him dreams that would come true—Joseph just had to trust.

My experiences have also made me realize how important it is to share my story with people. Because even when I was in trouble, even when I was facing blindness, even when I was facing criticism, and even when everything came crashing in on me, I still worked to trust God and keep His dreams for me in sight. God gave me that dream of walking across the stage on draft night, and that meant it would come true—even on days when I had my doubts.

And now God is doing it again with new dreams.

No matter what you might be facing today, I want you to promise me that you'll do this: Make it your story. Be positive and pray. Be willing to let God help you find ways to dream again. He did it for me—I am dreaming again. You can, too!

ACKNOWLEDGMENTS

FROM ISAIAH AUSTIN

I would like to thank my mom and dad; my brother, Noah; and my sister, Narah, for always being there for me. Thank you to Aunt Evelyn and Uncle Dre for everything you guys do for me.

I'd also like to thank Coach Ray. I wouldn't be the person I am without you, Coach. I'd like to thank Ray Sr. (Coach Pops) for all your prayers and good advice.

I'd like to thank my agent, Dwon Clifton, who helps keep my dream of inspiring people and bringing awareness to Marfan syndrome moving in the right direction.

I'd like to thank Coach Drew and each one of the guys on the Baylor staff for always supporting me and being here for me in my life after basketball. Thank you to all my Baylor teammates for supporting me through everything.

I need to thank all of my fans for the encouragement you've given me in good and bad times.

I want to thank the publishing team: all the people at Howard Books; my book agents, Matt and Sealy Yates; my writer, Matt Litton; and everyone involved with helping me tell my story.

Last, I want to thank everyone at the Marfan Foundation and my friends who are dealing with this syndrome for your prayers and support.

I hope you will take a minute to check out my efforts to bring awareness and raise money for Marfan research on the web: http://www.isaiahaustinfoundation.org.

I also hope you'll remember my story when you face adversity in your life. I hope I've inspired you to dream again.

FROM MATT LITTON

Basketball has been a huge part of my life since I was very young: as a player, later as a coach, and today mainly as a fan and father of four children who enjoy the game. So I began this project already familiar with Isaiah's story and as an admirer of his grit and determination as an athlete (and a person). I believed *Dream Again* would not only have a positive impact on readers, but would change (and even save) the lives of people who have to pick up the pieces of their own broken dreams.

I am very thankful to my family: Noah, Eli, Jake, Rae, and my wife, Kristy, whose enthusiasm for telling Isaiah's story matched my own. I love you all.

Thank you to my friend Kyle Olund, who always seems to be in the right place at the right time to help me out on my writing adventures.

I am grateful to Matt and Sealy Yates and to Isaiah for trusting me to write such a compelling story.

I'm thankful for the hospitality I was shown in Waco by Coach Scott Drew and the entire Baylor men's basketball program. I've never been around a team with a stronger sense of family, nor met coaches who care more deeply about their players.

As they say in Big XII country, "Sic 'em."

Before I first met Isaiah, I was told that Marfan syndrome had left him, in essence, with a "heart condition." When I first arrived at Baylor's gym, I watched Isaiah, the most talented basketball player on campus (likely any college campus), who was still grieving the recent news that he would never play ball again, on the floor wiping up his teammates' sweat during drills, running to grab water for them during breaks, pulling the younger players aside to encourage them, and setting the overall tone with his intense presence. I got to know a young man who is committed to being a servant leader and whose optimism and sense of humor lift up everyone around him. I don't know what challenges Marfan syndrome will bring him in the future, but let me tell you what I learned about Isaiah Austin's "heart condition": his heart is full of more joy, passion, and genuine faith than any young person I've ever met.

I am hopeful, no matter what adversity you come to face in your own life, that Isaiah's example will inspire you with the faith and tenacity to dream again.